St. Francis of Assisi

St. Francis of Assisi

G. K. Chesterton

CONTINUUM
London and New York

Continuum
The Tower Building, 11 York Road, London SE1 7NX
370 Lexington Avenue, New York, NY 10017–6503

© 2001 The Continuum International Publishing Company Ltd.

First published in 1924 by Hodder and Stoughton Ltd.
This edition published 2001 by Continuum

British Library Cataloguing-in-Publication Data
A catalogue record for this book is available from the British Library.

ISBN 0-8264-5421-6

Printed and bound in Great Britain by
Biddles Ltd, Guildford and King's Lynn

Contents

A SKETCH of St. Francis of Assisi in modern English may be written in one of three ways. Between these the writer must make his selection ; and the third way, which is adopted here, is in some respects the most difficult of all. At least, it would be the most difficult if the other two were not impossible.

First, he may deal with this great and most amazing man as a figure in secular history and a model of social virtues. He may describe this divine demagogue as being, as he probably was, the world's one quite sincere democrat. He may say (what means very little) that St. Francis was in advance of his age. He may say (what is quite true) that St. Francis anticipated all that is most liberal and sympathetic in the modern mood ; the love of nature ; the love of animals ; the sense of social compassion ; the sense of the spiritual dangers of prosperity and even of property. All those things that nobody understood before Wordsworth were familiar to St. Francis. All those things that were first discovered by Tolstoy had been taken for granted by St. Francis. He could be presented, not only as a human but a humanitarian hero; indeed as the first hero of humanism. He has been described as a sort of morning star of the Renaissance. And in comparison with all these things, his ascetical theology can be ignored or dismissed as a contemporary accident, which was fortunately not a fatal accident. His religion can be regarded as a superstition, but an inevitable superstition, from which not even genius could wholly free itself; in the consideration of which it would be unjust to condemn St. Francis for his self-denial or unduly chide him for his chastity. It is quite true that even from so detached a standpoint his stature would still appear heroic. There would still be a great deal to be said about the man who tried to end the Crusades by talking to the Saracens or who interceded with the Emperor for the birds. The writer might describe in a purely historical spirit the whole of that great Franciscan inspiration that was felt in the painting of Giotto, in the poetry of Dante, in the miracle plays that made possible the modern drama, and in so many other things that are already appreciated by the modern culture. He may try to do it, as others have done, almost without raising any religious question at all. In short, he may try to tell the story of a saint without God; which is like being told to write the life of Nansen and forbidden to mention the North Pole.

Second, he may go to the opposite extreme, and decide, as it were, to be defiantly devotional. He may make the theological enthusiasm as thoroughly the theme as it was the theme of the first Franciscans. He may treat religion as the real thing that it was to the real Francis of Assisi. He can find an austere joy, so to speak, in parading the paradoxes of asceticism and all the holy topsy-turvydom of humility. He can stamp the whole history with the Stigmata, record fasts like fights against a dragon; till in the vague modern mind St. Francis is as dark a figure as St. Dominic. In short he can produce what many in our world will regard as a sort of photographic negative, the reversal of all lights and shades; what the foolish will find as impenetrable as darkness and even many of the wise will find almost as invisible as if it were written in silver upon white. Such a study of St. Francis would be unintelligible to anyone who does not share his religion, perhaps only partly intelligible to anyone who does not share his vocation. According to degrees of judgment, it will be regarded as something too bad or too good for the world. The only difficulty about doing the thing in this way is that it cannot be done. It would really require a saint to write the life of a saint. In the present case the objections to such a course are insuperable.

Third, he may try to do what I have tried to do here; and, as I have already suggested, the course has peculiar problems of its own. The writer may put himself in the position of the ordinary modern outsider and enquirer; as indeed the present writer is still largely and was once entirely in that position. He may start from the standpoint of a man who already admires St. Francis, but only for those things which such a man finds admirable. In other words he may assume that the reader is at least as enlightened as Renan or Matthew Arnold; but in the light of that enlightenment he may try to illuminate what Renan and Matthew Arnold left dark. He may try to use what is understood to explain what is not understood. He may say to the modern English reader: " Here is an historical character which is admittedly attractive to many of us already, by its gaiety, its romantic imagination, its spiritual courtesy and camaraderie, but which also contains elements (evidently equally sincere and emphatic) which seem to you quite remote and repulsive. But after all, this man was a man and not half a dozen men. What seems inconsistency to you did not seem inconsistency to him. Let us see whether we can understand, with the help of the existing understanding, these other things that seem now to be doubly dark, by their intrinsic gloom and their ironic contrast." I do not mean, of course, that I can really reach such a pyschological completeness in this crude and curt outline. But I mean that this is the only controversial condition that I shall here assume; that I am dealing with the sympathetic outsider. I shall not assume any more or any less agreement than this. A materialist may not care whether the inconsistencies are reconciled or not. A Catholic may not see any inconsistencies to reconcile. But I am here addressing the ordinary modern man, sympathetic but sceptical, and I can only rather hazily hope that, by approaching the great saint's story through what is evidently picturesque and popular about it, I may at least leave the reader understanding a little more than he did before of the consistency of a complete character; that by approaching it in this way, we may at least get a glimmering of why the poet who praised his lord the sun, often hid himself in a dark cavern, of why the saint who was so gentle with his Brother the Wolf was so harsh to his Brother the Ass (as he nicknamed his own body), of why the troubadour who said that love set his heart on fire separated himself from women, of why the singer who rejoiced in the strength and gaiety of the fire deliberately rolled himself in the snow, of why the very song which cries with all the passion of a pagan, " Praised be God for our Sister, Mother Earth, which brings forth varied fruits and grass and glowing flowers," ends almost with the words " Praised be God for our Sister, the death of the body."

Renan and Matthew Arnold failed utterly at

this test. They were content to follow Francis with their praises until they were stopped by their prejudices; the stubborn prejudices of the sceptic. The moment Francis began to do something they did not understand or did not like, they did not try to understand it, still less to like it; they simply turned their backs on the whole business and " walked no more with him." No man will get any further along a path of historical enquiry in that fashion. These sceptics are really driven to drop the whole subject in despair, to leave the most simple and sincere of all historical characters as a mass of contradictions, to be praised on the principle of the curate's egg. Arnold refers to the asceticism of Alverno almost hurriedly, as if it were an unlucky but undeniable blot on the beauty of the story; or rather as if it were a pitiable break-down and bathos at the end of the story. Now this is simply to be stone-blind to the whole point of any story. To represent Mount Alverno as the mere collapse of Francis is exactly like representing Mount Calvary as the mere collapse of Christ. Those mountains are mountains, whatever else they are, and it is nonsense to say (like the Red Queen) that they are comparative hollows or negative holes in the ground. They were quite manifestly meant to be culminations and landmarks. To treat the Stigmata as a sort of scandal, to be touched on tenderly but with pain, is exactly like treating the original five wounds of Jesus Christ as five blots on His character. You may dislike the idea of asceticism; you may dislike equally the idea of martyrdom; for that matter you may have an honest and natural dislike of the whole conception of sacrifice symbolised by the cross. But if it is an intelligent dislike, you will still retain the capacity for seeing the point of a story; of the story of a martyr or even the story of a monk. You will not be able rationally to read the Gospel and regard the Crucifixion as an afterthought or an anti-climax or an accident in the life of Christ; it is obviously the point of the story like the point of a sword, the sword that pierced the heart of the Mother of God.

And you will not be able rationally to read the story of a man presented as a Mirror of Christ without understanding his final phase as a Man of Sorrows, and at least artistically appreciating the appropriateness of his receiving, in a cloud of mystery and isolation, inflicted by no human hand, the unhealed everlasting wounds that heal the world.

The practical reconciliation of the gaiety and austerity I must leave the story itself to suggest. But since I have mentioned Matthew Arnold and Renan and the rationalistic admirers of St. Francis, I will here give the hint of what it seems to me most advisable for such readers to keep in mind. These distinguished writers found things like the Stigmata a stumbling-

block because to them a religion was a philosophy.
It was an impersonal thing; and it is only the
most personal passion that provides here an
approximate earthly parallel. A man will not
roll in the snow for a stream of tendency by which
all things fulfil the law of their being. He will
not go without food in the name of something,
not ourselves, that makes for righteousness.
He will do things like this, or pretty nearly like
this, under quite a different impulse. He will
do these things when he is in love. The first
fact to realise about St. Francis is involved
in the first fact with which his story starts;
that when he said from the first that he was a
Troubadour, and said later that he was a Troubadour of a newer and nobler romance, he was
not using a mere metaphor, but understood
himself much better than the scholars understand
him. He was, to the last agonies of asceticism,
a Troubadour. He was a Lover. He was a
lover of God and he was really and truly a lover
of men; possibly a much rarer mystical vocation.
A lover of men is very nearly the opposite of a
philanthropist; indeed the pedantry of the Greek
word carries something like a satire on itself.
A philanthropist may be said to love anthropoids.
But as St. Francis did not love humanity but
men, so he did not love Christianity but Christ.
Say, if you think so, that he was a lunatic loving
an imaginary person; but an imaginary person,
not an imaginary idea. And for the modern

reader the clue to the asceticism and all the rest can best be found in the stories of lovers when they seemed to be rather like lunatics. Tell it as the tale of one of the Troubadours, and the wild things he would do for his lady, and the whole of the modern puzzle disappears. In such a romance there would be no contradiction between the poet gathering flowers in the sun and enduring a freezing vigil in the snow, between his praising all earthly and bodily beauty and then refusing to eat, between his glorifying gold and purple and perversely going in rags, between his showing pathetically a hunger for a happy life and a thirst for a heroic death. All these riddles would easily be resolved in the simplicity of any noble love; only this was so noble a love that nine men out of ten have hardly even heard of it. We shall see later that this parallel of the earthly lover has a very practical relation to the problems of his life, as to his relations with his father and with his friends and their families. The modern reader will almost always find that if he could only feel this kind of love as a reality, he could feel this kind of extravagance as a romance. But I only note it here as a preliminary point because, though it is very far from being the final truth in the matter, it is the best approach to it. The reader cannot even begin to see the sense of a story that may well seem to him a very wild one, until he under-stands that to this great mystic his religion was not a thing like a theory but a thing like a love-affair. And the only purpose of this prefatory chapter is to explain the limits of this present book; which is only addressed to that part of the modern world which finds in St. Francis a certain modern difficulty; which can admire him yet hardly accept him, or which can appreciate the saint almost without the sanctity. And my only claim even to attempt such a task is that I myself have for so long been in various stages of such a condition. Many thousand things that I now partly comprehend I should have thought utterly incomprehensible, many things I now hold sacred I should have scouted as utterly superstitious, many things that seem to me lucid and enlightened now they are seen from the inside I should honestly have called dark and barbarous seen from the outside, when long ago in those days of boyhood my fancy first caught fire with the glory of Francis of Assisi. I too have lived in Arcady; but even in Arcady I met one walking in a brown habit who loved the woods better than Pan. The figure in the brown habit stands above the hearth in the room where I write, and alone among many such images, at no stage of my pilgrimage has he ever seemed to me a stranger. There is something of harmony between the hearth and the firelight and my own first pleasure in his words about his brother fire; for he stands far enough back in my memory to mingle with all those more domestic dreams of the first days. Even the fantastic shadows thrown by fire make a sort of shadow pantomime that belongs to the nursery; yet the shadows were even then the shadows of his favourite beasts and birds, as he saw them, grotesque but haloed with the love of God. His Brother Wolf and Brother Sheep seemed then almost like the Brer Fox and Brer Rabbit of a more Christian Uncle Remus. I have come slowly to see many and more marvellous aspects of such a man, but I have never lost that one. His figure stands on a sort of bridge connecting my boyhood with my conversion to many other things; for the romance of his religion had penetrated even the rationalism of that vague Victorian time. In so far as I have had this experience, I may be able to lead others a little further along that road; but only a very little further. Nobody knows better than I do now that it is a road upon which angels might fear to tread; but though I am certain of failure I am not altogether overcome by fear; for he suffered fools gladly.

B

THE modern innovation which has substituted journalism for history, or for that tradition that is the gossip of history, has had at least one definite effect. It has insured that everybody should only hear the end of every story. Journalists are in the habit of printing above the very last chapters of their serial stories (when the hero and heroine are just about to embrace in the last chapter, as only an unfathomable perversity prevented them from doing in the first) the rather misleading words, " You can begin this story here." But even this is not a complete parallel; for the journals do give some sort of a summary of the story, while they never give anything remotely resembling a summary of the history. Newspapers not only deal with news, but they deal with everything as if it were entirely new. Tutankamen, for instance, was entirely new. It is exactly in the same fashion that we read that Admiral Bangs has been shot, which is the first intimation we have that he has ever been born. There is something singularly significant in the use which journalism makes of its stores of biography. It never thinks of publishing the life until it is publishing the death. As it deals with individuals it deals with institutions and ideas. After the Great War our public began to be told of all sorts of nations being emancipated. It had never been told a word about their being enslaved. We were called upon to judge of the justice of the settlements, when we had never been allowed to hear of the very existence of the quarrels. People would think it pedantic to talk about the Serbian epics and they prefer to speak in plain every-day modern language about the Yugo-Slavonic international new diplomacy; and they are quite excited about something they call Czecho-Slovakia without apparently having ever heard of Bohemia. Things that are as old as Europe are regarded as more recent than the very latest claims pegged out on the prairies of America. It is very exciting; like the last act of a play to people who have only come into the theatre just before the curtain falls. But it does not conduce exactly to knowing what it is all about. To those content with the mere fact of a pistol-shot or a passionate embrace, such a leisurely manner of patronising the drama may be recommended. To those tormented by a merely intellectual curiosity about who is kissing or killing whom, and why, it is unsatisfactory.

Most modern history, especially in England, suffers from the same imperfection as journalism. At best it only tells half of the history of Christendom; and that the second half without the first half. Men for whom reason begins with the Revival of Learning, men for whom religion begins with the Reformation, can never give a complete account of anything, for they have to start with institutions whose origin they cannot explain, or generally even imagine. Just as we hear of the admiral being shot but have never heard of his being born, so we all heard a great deal about the dissolution of the monasteries, but we heard next to nothing about the creation of the monasteries. Now this sort of history would be hopelessly insufficient, even for an intelligent man who hated the monasteries. It is hopelessly insufficient in connection with institutions that many intelligent men do in a quite healthy spirit hate. For instance, it is possible that some of us have occasionally seen some mention, by our learned leader-writers, of an obscure institution called the Spanish Inquisition. Well, it really is an obscure institution, according to them and the histories they read. It is obscure because its origin is obscure. Protestant history simply begins with the horrible thing in possession, as the pantomime begins with the demon king in the goblin kitchen. It is likely enough that it was, especially towards the end, a horrible thing that might be haunted by demons; but if we say this was so, we have no notion why it was so. To understand the Spanish Inquisition it would be necessary to discover two things that we have never dreamed of bothering about; what Spain was and what an Inquisition was. The former would bring in the whole great question about the Crusade against the Moors; and by what heroic chivalry a European nation freed itself of an alien domination from Africa. The latter would bring in the whole business of the other Crusade against the Albigensians, and why men loved and hated that nihilistic vision from Asia. Unless we understand that there was in these things originally the rush and romance of a Crusade, we cannot understand how they came to deceive men or drag them on towards evil. The Crusaders doubtless abused their victory, but there was a victory to abuse. And where there is victory there is valour in the field and popularity in the forum. There is some sort of enthusiasm that encourages excesses or covers faults. For instance, I for one have maintained from very early days the responsibility of the English for their atrocious treatment of the Irish. But it would be quite unfair to the English to describe even the devilry of '98 and leave out altogether all mention of the war with Napoleon. It would be unjust to suggest that the English mind was bent on nothing but the death of Emmett, when it was more probably full of the glory of the death of Nelson. Unfortunately '98 was very far from being the last date of such dirty work; and only a few years ago our politicians started trying to rule by random robbing and killing, while gently remonstrating with the

Irish for their memory of old unhappy far-off
things and battles long ago. But however badly
we may think of the Black-and-Tan business,
it would be unjust to forget that most of us were
not thinking of Black-and-Tan but of khaki; and
that khaki had just then a noble and national
connotation covering many things. To write
of the war in Ireland and leave out the war
against Prussia, and the English sincerity about
it, would be unjust to the English. So to talk
about the torture-engine as if it had been a
hideous toy is unjust to the Spanish. It does not
tell sensibly from the start the story of what the
Spaniard did, and why. We may concede to
our contemporaries that in any case it is not a
story that ends well. We do not insist that
in their version it should begin well. What we
complain of is that in their version it does not
begin at all. They are only in at the death;
or even, like Lord Tom Noddy, too late for the
hanging. It is quite true that it was sometimes
more horrible than any hanging; but they only
gather, so to speak, the very ashes of the ashes;
the fag-end of the faggot.

The case of the Inquisition is here taken at
random, for it is one among any number illustrating the same thing; and not because it is
especially connected with St. Francis, in whatever
sense it may have been connected with St.
Dominic. It may well be suggested later indeed
that St. Francis is unintelligible, just as St.

Dominic is unintelligible, unless we do understand something of what the thirteenth century meant by heresy and a crusade. But for the moment I use it as a lesser example for a much larger purpose. It is to point out that to begin the story of St. Francis with the birth of St. Francis would be to miss the whole point of the story, or rather not to tell the story at all. And it is to suggest that the modern tail-foremost type of journalistic history perpetually fails us. We learn about reformers without knowing what they had to reform, about rebels without a notion of what they rebelled against, of memorials that are not connected with any memory and restorations of things that had apparently never existed before. Even at the expense of this chapter appearing disproportionate, it is necessary to say something about the great movements that led up to the entrance of the founder of the Franciscans. It may seem to mean describing a world, or even a universe, in order to describe a man. It will inevitably mean that the world or the universe will be described with a few desperate generalisations in a few abrupt sentences. But so far from its meaning that we see a very small figure under so large a sky, it will mean that we must measure the sky before we can begin to measure the towering stature of the man.

And this phrase alone brings me to the preliminary suggestions that seem necessary before even a slight sketch of the life of St. Francis. It is necessary to realise, in however rude and elementary a fashion, into what sort of a world St. Francis entered and what has been the history of that world, at least in so far as it affected him. It is necessary to have, if only in a few sentences, a sort of preface in the form of an Outline of History, if we may borrow the phrase of Mr. Wells. In the case of Mr. Wells himself, it is evident that the distinguished novelist suffered the same disadvantage as if he had been obliged to write a novel of which he hated the hero. To write history and hate Rome, both pagan and papal, is practically to hate nearly everything that has happened. It comes very near to hating humanity on purely humanitarian grounds. To dislike both the priest and the soldier, both the laurels of the warrior and the lilies of the saint, is to suffer a division from the mass of mankind for which not all the dexterities of the finest and most flexible of modern intelligences can compensate. A much wider sympathy is needed for the historical setting of St. Francis, himself both a soldier and a saint. I will therefore conclude this chapter with a few generalisations about the world that St. Francis found.

Men will not believe because they will not broaden their minds. As a matter of individual belief, I should of course express it by saying that they are not sufficiently catholic to be Catholic. But I am not going to discuss here the doctrinal truths of Christianity, but simply the broad historical fact of Christianity, as it might appear to a really enlightened and imaginative person even if he were not a Christian. What I mean at the moment is that the majority of doubts are made out of details. In the course of random reading a man comes across a pagan custom that strikes him as picturesque or a Christian action that strikes him as cruel; but he does not enlarge his mind sufficiently to see the main truth about pagan custom or the Christian reaction against it. Until we understand, not necessarily in detail, but in their big bulk and proportion that pagan progress and that Christian reaction, we cannot really understand the point of history at which St. Francis appears or what his great popular mission was all about.

Now everybody knows, I imagine, that the twelfth and thirteenth centuries were an awakening of the world. They were a fresh flowering of culture and the creative arts after a long spell of much sterner and even more sterile experience which we call the Dark Ages. They may be called an emancipation; they were certainly an end; an end of what may at least seem a harsher and more inhuman time. But what was it that was ended? From what was it that men were emancipated? That is where there is a real collision and point at issue between the different philosophies of history. On the merely external and secular side, it has been truly said that men awoke from a sleep; but there had been dreams in that sleep of a mystical and sometimes of a monstrous kind. In that rationalistic routine into which most modern historians have fallen, it is considered enough to say that they were emancipated from mere savage superstition and advanced towards mere civilised enlightenment. Now this is the big blunder that stands as a stumbling-block at the very beginning of our story. Anybody who supposes that the Dark Ages were plain darkness and nothing else, and that the dawn of the thirteenth century was plain daylight and nothing else, will not be able to make head or tail of the human story of St. Francis of Assisi. The truth is that the joy of St. Francis and his Jongleurs de Dieu was not merely an awakening. It was something which cannot be understood without understanding their own mystical creed. The end of the Dark Ages was not merely the end of a sleep. It was certainly not merely the end of a superstitious enslavement. It was the end of something belonging to a quite definite but quite different order of ideas.

It was the end of a penance; or, if it be preferred, a purgation. It marked the moment when a certain spiritual expiation had been finally worked out and certain spiritual diseases had been finally expelled from the system. They had been expelled by an era of asceticism, which was the only thing that could have expelled them. Christianity had entered the world to cure the world; and she had cured it in the only way in which it could be cured.

Viewed merely in an external and experimental fashion, the whole of the high civilisation of antiquity had ended in the learning of a certain lesson; that is, in its conversion to Christianity. But that lesson was a psychological fact as well as a theological faith. That pagan civilisation had indeed been a very high civilisation. It would not weaken our thesis, it might even strengthen it, to say that it was the highest that humanity ever reached. It had discovered its still unrivalled arts of poetry and plastic representation; it had discovered its own permanent political ideals; it had discovered its own clear system of logic and of language. But above all, it had discovered its own mistake.

That mistake was too deep to be ideally defined; the short-hand of it is to call it the mistake of nature-worship. It might almost as truly be called the mistake of being natural; and it was a very natural mistake. The Greeks, the great guides and pioneers of pagan antiquity, started out with the idea of something splendidly obvious and direct; the idea that if man walked straight ahead on the high road of reason and nature, he could come to no harm; especially if he was, as the Greek was, eminently enlightened and intelligent. We might be so flippant as to say that man was simply to follow his nose, so long as it was a Greek nose. And the case of the Greeks themselves is alone enough to illustrate the strange but certain fatality that attends upon this fallacy. No sooner did the Greeks themselves begin to follow their own noses and their own notion of being natural, than the queerest thing in history seems to have happened to them. It was much too queer to be an easy matter to discuss. It may be remarked that our more repulsive realists never give us the benefit of their realism. Their studies of unsavoury subjects never take note of the testimony which they bear to the truths of a traditional morality. But if we had the taste for such things, we could cite thousands of such things as part of the case for Christian morals. And an instance of this is found in the fact that nobody has written, in this sense, a real moral history of the Greeks. Nobody has seen the scale or the strangeness of the story. The wisest men in the world set out to be natural; and the most unnatural thing in the world was the very first thing they did. The immediate effect of saluting the sun and the sunny sanity of nature was a perversion spreading like a pestilence. The greatest and even the purest philosophers could not apparently avoid this low sort of lunacy. Why? It would seem simple enough for the people whose poets had conceived Helen of Troy, whose sculptors had carved the Venus of Milo, to remain healthy on the point. The truth is that people who worship health cannot remain healthy. When Man goes straight he goes crooked. When he follows his nose he manages somehow to put his nose out of joint, or even to cut off his nose to spite his face; and that in accordance with something much deeper in human nature than nature-worshippers could ever understand. It was the discovery of that deeper thing, humanly speaking, that constituted the conversion to Christianity. There is a bias in man like the bias in the bowl; and Christianity was the discovery of how to correct the bias and therefore hit the mark. There are many who will smile at the saying; but it is profoundly true to say that the glad good news brought by the Gospel was the news of original sin.

Rome rose at the expense of her Greek teachers largely because she did not entirely consent to be taught these tricks. She had a much more decent domestic tradition; but she ultimately suffered from the same fallacy in her religious tradition; which was necessarily in no small degree the heathen tradition of nature-worship. What was the matter with the whole heathen civilisation was that there was nothing for the mass of men in the way of mysticism, except that concerned with the mystery of the nameless forces of nature, such as sex and growth and death. In the Roman Empire also, long before the end, we find nature-worship inevitably producing things that are against nature. Cases like that of Nero have passed into a proverb, when Sadism sat on a throne brazen in the broad daylight. But the truth I mean is something much more subtle and universal than a conventional catalogue of atrocities. What had happened to the human imagination, as a whole, was that the whole world was coloured by dangerous and rapidly deteriorating passions; by natural passions becoming unnatural passions. Thus the effect of treating sex as only one innocent natural thing was that every other innocent natural thing became soaked and sodden with sex. For sex cannot be admitted to a mere equality among elementary emotions or experiences like eating and sleeping. The moment sex ceases to be a servant it becomes a tyrant. There is something dangerous and disproportionate in its place in human nature, for whatever reason; and it does really need a special purification and dedication. The modern talk about sex being free like any other sense, about the body being beautiful like any tree or flower, is either a description of the Garden of Eden or a piece of thoroughly bad psychology, of which the world grew weary two thousand years ago.

This is not to be confused with mere self-righteous sensationalism about the wickedness of the pagan world. It was not so much that the pagan world was wicked as that it was good enough to realise that its paganism was becoming wicked, or rather was on the logical high road to wickedness. I mean that there was no future for " natural magic "; to deepen it was only to

darken it into black magic. There was no
future for it; because in the past it had only
been innocent because it was young. We might
say it had only been innocent because it was
shallow. Pagans were wiser than paganism;
that is why the pagans became Christians.
Thousands of them had philosophy and family
virtues and military honour to hold them up;
but by this time the purely popular thing called
religion was certainly dragging them down.
When this reaction against the evil is allowed
for, it is true to repeat that it was an evil that
was everywhere. In another and more literal
sense its name was Pan.

It was no metaphor to say that these people
needed a new heaven and a new earth; for they
had really defiled their own earth and even
their own heaven. How could their case be
met by looking at the sky, when erotic legends
were scrawled in stars across it; how could they
learn anything from the love of birds and flowers
after the sort of love stories that were told of
them? It is impossible here to multiply
evidences, and one small example may stand for
the rest. We know what sort of sentimental
associations are called up to us by the phrase
" a garden "; and how we think mostly of the
memory of melancholy and innocent romances,
or quite as often of some gracious maiden lady
or kindly old parson pottering under a yew hedge,
perhaps in sight of a village spire. Then, let

anyone who knows a little Latin poetry recall
suddenly what would once have stood in place
of the sun-dial or the fountain, obscene and
monstrous in the sun; and of what sort was
the god of their gardens.

Nothing could purge this obsession but a
religion that was literally unearthly. It was
no good telling such people to have a natural
religion full of stars and flowers; there was not
a flower or even a star that had not been stained.
They had to go into the desert where they
could find no flowers or even into the cavern
where they could see no stars. Into that desert
and that cavern the highest human intellect
entered for some four centuries; and it was
the very wisest thing it could do. Nothing but
the stark supernatural stood up for its salvation;
if God could not save it, certainly the gods
could not. The Early Church called the gods
of paganism devils; and the Early Church was
perfectly right. Whatever natural religion may
have had to do with their beginnings, nothing
but fiends now inhabited those hollow shrines.
Pan was nothing but panic. Venus was nothing
but venereal vice. I do not mean for a moment,
of course, that all the individual pagans were
of this character even to the end; but it was as
individuals that they differed from it. Nothing
distinguishes paganism from Christianity so
clearly as the fact that the individual thing
called philosophy had little or nothing to do with

the social thing called religion. Anyhow it was no good to preach natural religion to people to whom nature had grown as unnatural as any religion. They knew much better than we do what was the matter with them and what sort of demons at once tempted and tormented them; and they wrote across that great space of history the text: " This sort goeth not out but by prayer and fasting."

Now the historic importance of St. Francis and the transition from the twelfth to the thirteenth century, lies in the fact that they marked the end of this expiation. Men at the close of the Dark Ages may have been rude and unlettered and unlearned in everything but wars with heathen tribes, more barbarous than themselves, but they were clean. They were like children; the first beginnings of their rude arts have all the clean pleasure of children. We have to conceive them in Europe as a whole living under little local governments, feudal in so far as they were a survival of fierce wars with the barbarians, often monastic and carrying a more friendly and fatherly character, still faintly imperial in so far as Rome still ruled as a great legend. But in Italy something had survived more typical of the finer spirit of antiquity; the republic. Italy was dotted with little states, largely democratic in their ideals, and often filled with real citizens. But the city no longer lay open as under the Roman peace, but was pent in

c

high walls for defence against feudal war and all the citizens had to be soldiers. One of these stood in a steep and striking position on the wooded hills of Umbria; and its name was Assisi. Out of its deep gate under its high turrets was to come the message that was the gospel of the hour, " Your warfare is accomplished, your iniquity is pardoned." But it was out of all these fragmentary things of feudalism and freedom and remains of Roman Law that there was to rise, at the beginning of the thirteenth century, vast and almost universal, the mighty civilisation of the Middle Ages.

It is an exaggeration to attribute it entirely to the inspiration of any one man, even the most original genius of the thirteenth century. Its elementary ethics of fraternity and fair play had never been entirely extinct and Christendom had never been anything less than Christian. The great truisms about justice and pity can be found in the rudest monastic records of the barbaric transition or the stiffest maxims of the Byzantine decline. And early in the eleventh and twelfth centuries a larger moral movement had clearly begun. But what may fairly be said of it is this, that over all those first movements there was still something of that ancient austerity that came from the long penitential period. It was the twilight of morning; but it was still a grey twilight. This may be illustrated by the mere mention of two or three of

these reforms before the Franciscan reform.
The monastic institution itself, of course, was
far older than all these things; indeed it was
undoubtedly almost as old as Christianity.
Its counsels of perfection had always taken
the form of vows of chastity and poverty and
obedience. With these unworldly aims it had
long ago civilised a great part of the world.
The monks had taught people to plough and
sow as well as to read and write; indeed they
had taught the people nearly everything that
the people knew. But it may truly be said
that the monks were severely practical, in the
sense that they were not only practical but
also severe; though they were generally severe
with themselves and practical for other people.
All this early monastic movement had long ago
settled down and doubtless often deteriorated;
but when we come to the first medieval movements this sterner character is still apparent.
Three examples may be taken to illustrate the
point.

First, the ancient social mould of slavery
was already beginning to melt. Not only was
the slave turning into the serf, who was practically
free as regards his own farm and family life,
but many lords were freeing slaves and serfs
altogether. This was done under the pressure
of the priests; but especially it was done in the
spirit of a penance. In one sense, of course,
any Catholic society must have an atmosphere

of penance; but I am speaking of that rather sterner spirit of penance which had expiated the excesses of paganism. There was about such restitutions the atmosphere of the death-bed; as many of them doubtless were examples of death-bed repentance. A very honest atheist with whom I once debated made use of the expression, " Men have only been kept in slavery by the fear of hell." As I pointed out to him, if he had said that men had only been freed from slavery by the fear of hell, he would at least have been referring to an unquestionable historical fact.

Another example was the sweeping reform of Church discipline by Pope Gregory the Seventh. It really was a reform, undertaken from the highest motives and having the healthiest results; it conducted a searching inquisition against simony or the financial corruptions of the clergy; it insisted on a more serious and self-sacrificing ideal for the life of a parish priest. But the very fact that this largely took the form of making universal the obligation of celibacy will strike the note of something which, however noble, would seem to many to be vaguely negative. The third example is in one sense the strongest of all. For the third example was a war; a heroic war and for many of us a holy war; but still something having all the stark and terrible responsibilities of war. There is no space here to say all that should be said about the true nature of the Crusades. Everybody knows that in the very darkest hour of the Dark Ages a sort of heresy had sprung up in Arabia and become a new religion of a military but nomadic sort, invoking the name of Mahomet. Intrinsically it had a character found in many heresies from the Moslem to the Monist. It seemed to the heretic a sane simplification of religion; while it seems to the Catholic an insane simplification of religion, because it simplifies all to a single idea and so loses the breadth and balance of Catholicism. Anyhow its objective character was that of a military danger to Christendom and Christendom had struck at the very heart of it, in seeking to reconquer the Holy Places. The great Duke Godfrey and the first Christians who stormed Jerusalem were heroes if there were ever any in the world; but they were the heroes of a tragedy.

Now I have taken these two or three examples of the earlier medieval movements in order to note about them one general character, which refers back to the penance that followed paganism. There is something in all these movements that is bracing even while it is still bleak, like a wind blowing between the clefts of the mountains. That wind, austere and pure, of which the poet speaks, is really the spirit of the time, for it is the wind of a world that has at last been purified. To anyone who can appreciate atmospheres there is something clear and clean about the atmosphere of this crude and often harsh society. Its very lusts are clean; for they have no longer any smell of perversion. Its very cruelties are clean; they are not the luxurious cruelties of the amphitheatre. They come either of a very simple horror at blasphemy or a very simple fury at insult. Gradually against this grey background beauty begins to appear, as something really fresh and delicate and above all surprising. Love returning is no longer what was once called platonic but what is still called chivalric love. The flowers and stars have recovered their first innocence. Fire and water are felt to be worthy to be the brother and sister of a saint. The purge of paganism is complete at last.

For water itself has been washed. Fire itself has been purified as by fire. Water is no longer that water into which slaves were flung to feed the fishes. Fire is no longer that fire through which children were passed to Moloch. Flowers smell no more of the forgotten garlands gathered in the garden of Priapus; stars stand no more as signs of the far frigidity of gods as cold as those cold fires. They are all like things newly made and awaiting new names, from one who shall come to name them. Neither the universe nor the earth have now any longer the old sinister significance of the world. They await a new reconciliation with man, but they are already capable of being reconciled. Man has stripped from his soul the last rag of nature-worship, and can return to nature.

While it was yet twilight a figure appeared silently and suddenly on a little hill above the city, dark against the fading darkness. For it was the end of a long and stern night, a night of vigil, not unvisited by stars. He stood with his hands lifted, as in so many statues and pictures, and about him was a burst of birds singing; and behind him was the break of day.

ACCORDING to one tale, which if not true would be none the less typical, the very name of St. Francis was not so much a name as a nickname. There would be something akin to his familiar and popular instinct in the notion that he was nicknamed very much as an ordinary schoolboy might be called " Frenchy " at school. According to this version, his name was not Francis at all but John; and his companions called him " Francesco " or " The little Frenchman " because of his passion for the French poetry of the Troubadours. The more probable story is that his mother had named him John when he was born in the absence of his father, who shortly returned from a visit to France, where his commercial success had filled him with so much enthusiasm for French taste and social usage that he gave his son the new name signifying the Frank or Frenchman In either case the name has a certain significance, as connecting Francis from the first with what he himself regarded as the romantic fairyland of the Troubadours.

The name of the father was Pietro Bernardone and he was a substantial citizen of the guild of the cloth merchants in the town of Assisi. It is hard to describe the position of such a man without some appreciation of the position of such a guild and even of such a town. It did not exactly correspond to anything that is meant in modern times either by a merchant or a man of business or a tradesman, or anything that exists under the conditions of capitalism. Bernardone may have employed people but he was not an employer; that is, he did not belong to an employing class as distinct from an employed class. The person we definitely hear of his employing is his son Francis; who, one is tempted to guess, was about the last person that any man of business would employ if it were convenient to employ anybody else. He was rich, as a peasant may be rich by the work of his own family; but he evidently expected his own family to work in a way almost as plain as a peasant's. He was a prominent citizen, but he belonged to a social order which existed to prevent him being too prominent to be a citizen. It kept all such people on their own simple level, and no prosperity connoted that escape from drudgery by which in modern times the lad might have seemed to be a lord or a fine gentleman or something other than the cloth merchant's son. This is a rule that is proved even in the exception. Francis was one of those people who are popular with everybody in any case; and his guileless swagger as a Troubadour and leader of French

fashions made him a sort of romantic ringleader
among the young men of the town. He threw
money about both in extravagance and bene-
volence, in a way native to a man who never,
all his life, exactly understood what money was.
This moved his mother to mingled exultation
and exasperation and she said, as any tradesman's
wife might say anywhere : " He is more like a
prince than our son." But one of the earliest
glimpses we have of him shows him as simply
selling bales of cloth from a booth in the market;
which his mother may or may not have believed
to be one of the habits of princes. This first
glimpse of the young man in the market is symbolic in more ways than one. An incident
occurred which is perhaps the shortest and sharpest
summary that could be given of certain curious
things which were a part of his character, long
before it was transfigured by transcendental
faith. While he was selling velvet and fine
embroideries to some solid merchant of the town,
a beggar came imploring alms; evidently in a
somewhat tactless manner. It was a rude and
simple society and there were no laws to punish
a starving man for expressing his need for food,
such as have been established in a more humanitarian age; and the lack of any organised police
permitted such persons to pester the wealthy
without any great danger. But there was, I
believe, in many places a local custom of the guild
forbidding outsiders to interrupt a fair bargain;

and it is possible that some such thing put the mendicant more than normally in the wrong. Francis had all his life a great liking for people who had been put hopelessly in the wrong. On this occasion he seems to have dealt with the double interview with rather a divided mind; certainly with distraction, possibly with irritation. Perhaps he was all the more uneasy because of the almost fastidious standard of manners that came to him quite naturally. All are agreed that politeness flowed from him from the first, like one of the public fountains in such a sunny Italian market place. He might have written among his own poems as his own motto that verse of Mr. Belloc's poem—

> ' Of Courtesy, it is much less
> Than courage of heart or holiness,
> Yet in my walks it seems to me
> That the grace of God is in Courtesy.'

Nobody ever doubted that Francis Bernardone had courage of heart, even of the most ordinary manly and military sort; and a time was to come when there was quite as little doubt about the holiness and the grace of God. But I think that if there was one thing about which he was punctilious, it was punctiliousness. If there was one thing of which so humble a man could be said to be proud, he was proud of good manners. Only behind his perfectly natural urbanity were wider and even wilder possibilities, of which we get the first flash in this trivial incident. Anyhow

Francis was evidently torn two ways with the botheration of two talkers, but finished his business with the merchant somehow; and when he had finished it, found the beggar was gone. Francis leapt from his booth, left all the bales of velvet and embroidery behind him apparently unprotected, and went racing across the market-place like an arrow from the bow. Still running, he threaded the labyrinth of the narrow and crooked streets of the little town, looking for his beggar, whom he eventually discovered; and loaded that astonished mendicant with money. Then he straightened himself, so to speak, and swore before God that he would never all his life refuse help to a poor man. The sweeping simplicity of this undertaking is extremely characteristic. Never was any man so little afraid of his own promises. His life was one riot of rash vows; of rash vows that turned out right.

The first biographers of Francis, naturally alive with the great religious revolution that he wrought, equally naturally looked back to his first years chiefly for omens and signs of such a spiritual earthquake. But writing at a greater distance, we shall not decrease that dramatic effect, but rather increase it, if we realise that there was not at this time any external sign of anything particularly mystical about the young man. He had not anything of that early sense of his vocation that has belonged to some of the saints. Over and above his main ambition to win fame as a French poet, he would seem to have most often thought of winning fame as a soldier. He was born kind; he was brave in the normal boyish fashion; but he drew the line both in kindness and bravery pretty well where most boys would have drawn it; for instance, he had the human horror of leprosy of which few normal people felt any need to be ashamed. He had the love of gay and bright apparel which was inherent in the heraldic taste of medieval times and seems altogether to have been rather a festive figure. If he did not paint the town red, he would probably have preferred to paint it all the colours of the rainbow, as in a medieval picture. But in this story of the young man in gay garments scampering after the vanishing beggar in rags there are certain notes of his natural individuality that must be assumed from first to last.

For instance, there is the spirit of swiftness. In a sense he continued running for the rest of his life, as he ran after the beggar. Because nearly all the errands he ran on were errands of mercy, there appeared in his portraiture a mere element of mildness which was true in the truest sense, but is easily misunderstood. A certain precipitancy was the very poise of his soul. This saint should be represented among the other saints as angels were sometimes represented in pictures of angels; with flying feet or even with feathers; in the spirit of the text that makes

angels winds and messengers a flaming fire. It
is a curiosity of language that courage actually
means running; and some of our sceptics will no
doubt demonstrate that courage really means
running away. But his courage was running,
in the sense of rushing. With all his gentleness,
there was originally something of impatience in
his impetuosity. The psychological truth about
it illustrates very well the modern muddle
about the word " practical." If we mean by
what is practical what is most immediately
practicable, we mean merely what is easiest. In
that sense St. Francis was very unpractical,
and his ultimate aims were very unworldly. But
if we mean by practicality a preference for prompt
effort and energy over doubt or delay, he was very
practical indeed. Some might call him a madman,
but he was the very reverse of a dreamer. Nobody
would be likely to call him a man of business;
but he was very emphatically a man of action.
In some of his early experiments he was rather
too much of a man of action; he acted too soon
and was too practical to be prudent. But at every
turn of his extraordinary career we shall find him
flinging himself round corners in the most unexpected fashion, as when he flew through the
crooked streets after the beggar.

Another element implied in the story, which
was already partially a natural instinct, before
it became a supernatural ideal, was something

that had never perhaps been wholly lost in those little republics of medieval Italy. It was something very puzzling to some people; something clearer as a rule to Southerners than to Northerners, and I think to Catholics than to Protestants; the quite natural assumption of the equality of men. It has nothing necessarily to do with the Franciscan love for men; on the contrary one of its merely practical tests is the equality of the duel. Perhaps a gentleman will never be fully an egalitarian until he can really quarrel with his servant. But it was an antecedent condition of the Franciscan brotherhood; and we feel it in this early and secular incident. Francis, I fancy, felt a real doubt about which he must attend to, the beggar or the merchant; and having attended to the merchant, he turned to attend to the beggar; he thought of them as two men. This is a thing much more difficult to describe, in a society from which it is absent, but it was the original basis of the whole business; it was why the popular movement arose in that sort of place and that sort of man. His imaginative magnanimity afterwards rose like a tower to starry heights that might well seem dizzy and even crazy; but it was founded on this high table-land of human equality.

I have taken this the first among a hundred tales of the youth of St. Francis, and dwelt on its significance a little, because until we have learned to look for the significance there will often seem to be little but a sort of light sentiment in telling the story. St. Francis is not a proper person to be patronised with merely " pretty " stories. There are any number of them; but they are too often used so as to be a sort of sentimental sediment of the medieval world, instead of being, as the saint emphatically is, a challenge to the modern world. We must take his real human development somewhat more seriously; and the next story in which we get a real glimpse of it is in a very different setting. But in exactly the same way it opens, as if by accident, certain abysses of the mind and perhaps of the unconscious mind. Francis still looks more or less like an ordinary young man; and it is only when we look at him as an ordinary young man, that we realise what an extraordinary young man he must be.

War had broken out between Assisi and Perugia. It is now fashionable to say in a satirical spirit that such wars did not so much break out as go on indefinitely between the city-states of medieval Italy. It will be enough to say here that if one of these medieval wars had really gone on without stopping for a century, it might possibly have come within a remote distance of killing as many people as we kill in a year, in one of our great modern scientific wars between our great modern industrial empires. But the citizens of the medieval republic were certainly under the limitation of only being asked to die for the things with which they had always lived, the houses they inhabited, the shrines they venerated and the rulers and representatives they knew; and had not the larger vision calling them to die for the latest rumours about remote colonies as reported in anonymous newspapers. And if we infer from our own experience that war paralysed civilisation, we must at least admit that these warring towns turned out a number of paralytics who go by the names of Dante and Michael Angelo, Ariosto and Titian, Leonardo and Columbus, not to mention Catherine of Siena and the subject of this story. While we lament all this local patriotism as a hubbub of the Dark Ages, it must seem a rather curious fact that about three quarters of the greatest men who ever lived came out of these little towns and were often engaged in these little wars. It remains to be seen what will ultimately come out of our large towns; but there has been no sign of anything of this sort since they became large; and I have sometimes been haunted by a fancy of my youth, that these things will not come till there is a city wall round Clapham and the tocsin is rung at night to arm the citizens of Wimbledon.

Anyhow, the tocsin was rung in Assisi and the citizens armed, and among them Francis the son of the cloth merchant. He went out to fight

D

with some company of lancers and in some fight
or foray or other he and his little band were taken
prisoners. To me it seems most probable that
there had been some tale of treason or cowardice
about the disaster; for we are told that there
was one of the captives with whom his fellow-
prisoners flatly refused to associate even in prison;
and when this happens in such circumstances, it
is generally because the military blame for the
surrender is thrown on some individual. Anyhow, somebody noted a small but curious thing,
though it might seem rather negative than positive. Francis, we are told, moved among his
captive companions with all his characteristic
courtesy and even conviviality, "liberal and
hilarious" as somebody said of him, resolved to
keep up their spirits and his own. And when
he came across the mysterious outcast, traitor
or coward or whatever he was called, he simply
treated him exactly like all the rest, neither with
coldness nor compassion, but with the same
unaffected gaiety and good fellowship. But if
there had been present in that prison someone
with a sort of second sight about the truth and
trend of spiritual things, he might have known
he was in the presence of something new and seemingly almost anarchic; a deep tide driving
out to uncharted seas of charity. For in this
sense there was really something wanting in
Francis of Assisi, something to which he was

blind that he might see better and more beautiful
things. All those limits in good fellowship and
good form, all those landmarks of social life that
divide the tolerable and the intolerable, all those
social scruples and conventional conditions that
are normal and even noble in ordinary men, all
those things that hold many decent societies
together, could never hold this man at all. He
liked as he liked; he seems to have liked everybody, but especially those whom everybody
disliked him for liking. Something very vast
and universal was already present in that narrow
dungeon; and such a seer might have seen in
its darkness that red halo of *caritas caritatum*
which marks one saint among saints as well as
among men. He might have heard the first
whisper of that wild blessing that afterwards
took the form of a blasphemy; " He listens to
those to whom God himself will not listen."

But though such a seer might have seen such
a truth, it is exceedingly doubtful if Francis
himself saw it. He had acted out of an unconscious
largeness, or in the fine medieval phrase largesse,
within himself, something that might almost
have been lawless if it had not been reaching out
to a more divine law; but it is doubtful whether
he yet knew that the law was divine. It is
evident that he had not at this time any notion
of abandoning the military, still less of adopting
the monastic life. It is true that there is not,

as pacifists and prigs imagine, the least inconsistency between loving men and fighting them, if
we fight them fairly and for a good cause.   But
it seems to me that there was more than this
involved; that the mind of the young man was
really running towards a military morality in
any case.   About this time the first calamity
crossed his path in the form of a malady which
was to revisit him many times and hamper his
headlong career.   Sickness made him more serious;
but one fancies it would only have made him
a more serious soldier, or even more serious about
soldiering.   And while he was recovering, something rather larger than the little feuds and raids
of the Italian towns opened an avenue of adventure
and ambition.   The crown of Sicily, a considerable centre of controversy at the time, was apparently claimed by a certain Gauthier de Brienne,
and the Papal cause to aid which Gauthier was
called in aroused enthusiasm among a number
of young Assisians, including Francis, who proposed to march into Apulia on the count's behalf;
perhaps his French name had something to do
with it.   For it must never be forgotten that
though that world was in one sense a world of
little things, it was a world of little things concerned about great things.   There was more
internationalism in the lands dotted with tiny
republics than in the huge homogeneous impenetrable national divisions of to-day.   The legal

authority of the Assisian magistrates might hardly reach further than a bow-shot from their high embattled city walls. But their sympathies might be with the ride of the Normans through Sicily or the palace of the Troubadours at Toulouse ; with the Emperor throned in the German forests or the great Pope dying in the exile of Salerno. Above all, it must be remembered that when the interests of an age are mainly religious they must be universal. Nothing can be more universal than the universe. And there are several things about the religious position at that particular moment which modern people not unnaturally fail to realise. For one thing, modern people naturally think of people so remote as ancient people, and even early people. We feel vaguely that these things happened in the first ages of the Church. The Church was already a good deal more than a thousand years old. That is, the Church was then rather older than France is now, a great deal older than England is now. And she looked old then ; almost as old as she does now ; possibly older than she does now. The Church looked like great Charlemagne with the long white beard, who had already fought a hundred wars with the heathen, and in the legend was bidden by an angel to go forth and fight once more though he was two hundred years old. The Church had topped her thousand years and turned the corner of the second thousand ; she had come through the Dark Ages in which nothing could be done except desperate fighting against the barbarians and the stubborn repetition of the creed. The creed was still being repeated after the victory or escape; but it is not unnatural to suppose that there was something a little monotonous about the repetition. The Church looked old then as now; and there were some who thought her dying then as now. In truth orthodoxy was not dead but it may have been dull; it is certain that some people began to think it dull. The Troubadours of the Provençal movement had already begun to take that turn or twist towards Oriental fancies and the paradox of pessimism, which always come to Europeans as something fresh when their own sanity seems to be something stale. It is likely enough that after all those centuries of hopeless war without and ruthless asceticism within, the official orthodoxy seemed to be something stale. The freshness and freedom of the first Christians seemed then as much as now a lost and almost prehistoric age of gold. Rome was still more rational than anything else; the Church was really wiser but it may well have seemed wearier than the world. There was something more adventurous and alluring, perhaps, about the mad metaphysics that had been blown across out of Asia. Dreams were gathering like dark clouds over the Midi to break in a thunder of anathema and civil war.

Only the light lay on the great plain round Rome;
but the light was blank and the plain was flat;
and there was no stir in the still air and the immemorial silence about the sacred town.

High in the dark house of Assisi Francesco
Bernardone slept and dreamed of arms. There
came to him in the darkness a vision splendid
with swords, patterned after the cross in the
Crusading fashion, of spears and shields and helmets
hung in a high armoury, all bearing the sacred
sign. When he awoke he accepted the dream
as a trumpet bidding him to the battlefield, and
rushed out to take horse and arms. He delighted
in all the exercises of chivalry; and was evidently
an accomplished cavalier and fighting man by
the tests of the tournament and the camp. He
would doubtless at any time have preferred a
Christian sort of chivalry; but it seems clear
that he was also in a mood which thirsted for
glory, though in him that glory would always
have been identical with honour. He was not
without some vision of that wreath of laurel
which Cæsar has left for all the Latins. As he
rode out to war the great gate in the deep wall
of Assisi resounded with his last boast, " I shall
come back a great prince."

A little way along his road his sickness rose
again and threw him. It seems highly probable,
in the light of his impetuous temper, that he had
ridden away long before he was fit to move. And

in the darkness of this second and far more
desolating interruption, he seems to have had
another dream in which a voice said to him,
" You have mistaken the meaning of the vision.
Return to your own town." And Francis trailed
back in his sickness to Assisi, a very dismal and
disappointed and perhaps even derided figure,
with nothing to do but to wait for what should
happen next. It was his first descent into a dark
ravine that is called the valley of humiliation,
which seemed to him very rocky and desolate,
but in which he was afterwards to find many
flowers.

But he was not only disappointed and humili-
ated; he was also very much puzzled and bewildered. He still firmly believed that his two dreams
must have meant something; and he could not
imagine what they could possibly mean. It was
while he was drifting, one may even say mooning,
about the streets of Assisi and the fields outside
the city wall, that an incident occurred to him
which has not always been immediately connected
with the business of the dreams, but which seems
to me the obvious culmination of them. He
was riding listlessly in some wayside place, apparently in the open country, when he saw a figure
coming along the road towards him and halted;
for he saw it was a leper. And he knew instantly
that his courage was challenged, not as the world
challenges, but as one would challenge who knew

the secrets of the heart of a man. What he saw advancing was not the banner and spears of Perugia, from which it never occurred to him to shrink; not the armies that fought for the crown of Sicily, of which he had always thought as a courageous man thinks of mere vulgar danger. Francis Bernardone saw his fear coming up the road towards him; the fear that comes from within and not without; though it stood white and horrible in the sunlight. For once in the long rush of his life his soul must have stood still. Then he sprang from his horse, knowing nothing between stillness and swiftness, and rushed on the leper and threw his arms round him. It was the beginning of a long vocation of ministry among many lepers, for whom he did many services; to this man he gave what money he could and mounted and rode on. We do not know how far he rode, or with what sense of the things around him; but it is said that when he looked back, he could see no figure on the road.

WE have now reached the great break in the life of Francis of Assisi; the point at which something happened to him that must remain greatly dark to most of us, who are ordinary and selfish men whom God has not broken to make anew.

In dealing with this difficult passage, especially for my own purpose of making things moderately easy for the more secular sympathiser, I have hesitated as to the proper course; and have eventually decided to state first of all what happened, with little more than a hint of what I imagine to have been the meaning of what happened. The fuller meaning may be debated more easily afterwards, when it was unfolded in the full Franciscan life. Anyhow what happened was this. The story very largely revolves round the ruins of the Church of St. Damian, an old shrine in Assisi which was apparently neglected and falling to pieces. Here Francis was in the habit of praying before the crucifix during these dark and aimless days of transition that followed the tragical collapse of all his military ambitions, probably made bitter by some loss of social prestige terrible to his sensitive spirit. As he did so he heard a voice saying to him, " Francis, seest thou not that my house is in ruins? Go and restore it for me."

Francis sprang up and went. To go and do something was one of the driving demands of his nature; probably he had gone and done it before he had at all thoroughly thought out what he had done. In any case what he had done was something very decisive and immediately very disastrous for his singular social career. In the coarse conventional language of the uncomprehending world, he stole. From his own enthusiastic point of view, he extended to his venerable father Peter Bernardone the exquisite excitement and inestimable privilege of assisting, more or less unconsciously, in the rebuilding of St. Damian's Church. In point of fact what he did was first to sell his own horse and then to go off and sell several bales of his father's cloth, making the sign of the cross over them to indicate their pious and charitable destination. Peter Bernardone did not see things in this light. Peter Bernardone indeed had not very much light to see by, so far as understanding the genius and temperament of his extraordinary son was concerned. Instead of understanding

in what sort of a wind and flame of abstract
appetites the lad was living, instead of simply
telling him (as the priest practically did later)
that he had done an indefensible thing with the
best intentions, old Bernardone took up the
matter in the hardest style; in a legal and
literal fashion. He used absolute political powers
like a heathen father, and himself put his son under
lock and key as a vulgar thief. It would appear
that the cry was caught up among many with
whom the unlucky Francis had once been popular;
and altogether, in his efforts to build up the
house of God he had only succeeded in bringing
his own house about his ears and lying buried
under the ruins. The quarrel dragged drearily
through several stages; at one time the wretched
young man seems to have disappeared under-
ground, so to speak, into some cavern or cellar
where he remained huddled hopelessly in the
darkness. Anyhow, it was his blackest moment;
the whole world had turned over; the whole
world was on top of him.

When he came out, it was only perhaps
gradually that anybody grasped that something
had happened. He and his father were summoned in the court of the bishop; for Francis
had refused the authority of all legal tribunals.
The bishop addressed some remarks to him,
full of that excellent common sense which the
Catholic Church keeps permanently as the back-

ground for all the fiery attitudes of her saints. He told Francis that he must unquestionably restore the money to his father; that no blessing could follow a good work done by unjust methods; and in short (to put it crudely) if the young fanatic would give back his money to the old fool, the incident would then terminate. There was a new air about Francis. He was no longer crushed, still less crawling, so far as his father was concerned; yet his words do not, I think, indicate either just indignation or wanton insult or anything in the nature of a mere continuation of the quarrel. They are rather remotely akin to mysterious utterances of his great model, " What have I to do with thee? " or even the terrible " Touch me not."

He stood up before them all and said, " Up to this time I have called Pietro Bernardone father, but now I am the servant of God. Not only the money but everything that can be called his I will restore to my father, even the very clothes he has given me." And he rent off all his garments except one; and they saw that that was a hair-shirt.

He piled the garments in a heap on the floor and tossed the money on top of them. Then he turned to the bishop, and received his blessing, like one who turns his back on society; and, according to the account, went out as he was into the cold world. Apparently it was literally

a cold world at the moment, and snow was on
the ground. A curious detail, very deep in its
significance, I fancy, is given in the same account
of this great crisis in his life. He went out
half-naked in his hair-shirt into the winter
woods, walking the frozen ground between the
frosty trees; a man without a father. He was
penniless, he was parentless, he was to all appearance without a trade or a plan or a hope in the
world; and as he went under the frosty trees,
he burst suddenly into song.

It was apparently noted as remarkable that
the language in which he sang was French,
or that Provençal which was called for convenience French. It was not his native language;
and it was in his native language that he
ultimately won fame as a poet; indeed St.
Francis is one of the very first of the national
poets in the purely national dialects of Europe.
But it was the language with which all his most
boyish ardours and ambitions had been iden-
tified; it was for him pre-eminently the language
of romance. That it broke from him in this
extraordinary extremity seems to me something
at first sight very strange and in the last analysis
very significant. What that significance was,
or may well have been, I will try to suggest in
the subsequent chapter; it is enough to indicate
here that the whole philosophy of St. Francis
revolved round the idea of a new supernatural

light on natural things, which meant the ultimate recovery not the ultimate refusal of natural things. And for the purpose of this purely narrative part of the business, it is enough to record that while he wandered in the winter forest in his hair-shirt, like the very wildest of the hermits, he sang in the tongue of the Troubadours.

Meanwhile the narrative naturally reverts to the problem of the ruined or at least neglected church, which had been the starting point of the saint's innocent crime and beatific punishment. That problem still predominated in his mind and was soon engaging his insatiable activities; but they were activities of a new sort; and he made no more attempts to interfere with the commercial ethics of the town of Assisi. There had dawned on him one of those great paradoxes that are also platitudes. He realised that the way to build a church is not to become entangled in bargains and, to him, rather bewildering questions of legal claim. The way to build a church is not to pay for it, certainly not with somebody else's money. The way to build a church is not even to pay for it with your own money. The way to build a church is to build it.

He went about by himself collecting stones. He begged all the people he met to give him stones. In fact he became a new sort of beggar, reversing the parable; a beggar who asks not for bread but a stone. Probably, as happened to him again and again throughout his extraordinary existence, the very queerness of the request gave it a sort of popularity; and all sorts of idle and luxurious people fell in with the benevolent project, as they would have done with a bet. He worked with his own hands at the rebuilding of the church, dragging the material like a beast of burden and learning the very last and lowest lessons of toil. A vast number of stories are told about Francis at this as at every other period of his life; but for the purpose here, which is one of simplification, it is best to dwell on this definite re-entrance of the saint into the world by the low gate of manual labour. There does indeed run through the whole of his life a sort of double meaning, like his shadow thrown upon the wall. All his action had something of the character of an allegory; and it is likely enough that some leaden-witted scientific historian may some day try to prove that he himself was never anything but an allegory. It is true enough in this sense that he was labouring at a double task, and rebuilding something else as well as the church of St. Damian. He was not only discovering the general lesson that his glory was not to be in overthrowing men in battle but in building up the positive and creative monuments of peace. He was truly building up something else, or beginning to build it up; something that has often enough fallen into ruin but has never been past rebuilding; a church that could always be built anew though it had rotted away to its first foundation-stone, against which the gates of hell shall not prevail.

The next stage in his progress is probably marked by his transferring the same energies of architectural reconstruction to the little church of St. Mary of the Angels at the Portiuncula. He had already done something of the same kind at a church dedicated to St. Peter; and that quality in his life noted above, which made it seem like a symbolical drama, led many of his most devout biographers to note the numerical symbolism of the three churches. There was at any rate a more historical and practical symbolism about two of them. For the original church of St. Damian afterwards became the seat of his striking experiment of a female order, and of the pure and spiritual romance of St. Clare. And the church of the Portiuncula will remain for ever as one of the great historic buildings of the world; for it was there that he gathered the little knot of friends and enthusiasts; it was the home of many homeless men. At this time, however, it is not clear that he had the definite idea of any such monastic developments. How early the plan appeared in his own mind

E

it is of course impossible to say; but on the face of events it first takes the form of a few friends who attached themselves to him one by one because they shared his own passion for simplicity. The account given of the form of their dedication is, however, very significant; for it was that of an invocation of the simplification of life as suggested in the New Testament. The adoration of Christ had been a part of the man's passionate nature for a long time past. But the imitation of Christ, as a sort of plan or ordered scheme of life, may in that sense be said to begin here.

The two men who have the credit, apparently, of having first perceived something of what was happening in the world of the soul were a solid and wealthy citizen named Bernard of Quintavalle and a canon from a neighbouring church named Peter. It is the more to their credit because Francis, if one may put it so, was by this time wallowing in poverty and association with lepers and ragged mendicants; and these two were men with much to give up; the one of comforts in the world and the other of ambition in the Church. Bernard the rich burgher did quite literally and finally sell all he had and give to the poor. Peter did even more; for he descended from a chair of spiritual authority, probably when he was already a man of mature years and therefore of fixed mental habits, to follow an extravagant young eccentric whom most people probably regarded as a maniac What it was of which they had caught a glimpse, of which Francis had seen the glory, may be suggested later so far as it can be suggested at all. At this stage we need profess to see no more than all Assisi saw, and that something not altogether unworthy of comment. The citizens of Assisi only saw the camel go in triumph through the eye of the needle and God doing impossible things because to him all things were possible; only a priest who rent his robes like the Publican and not like the Pharisee and a rich man who went away joyful, for he had no possessions.

These three strange figures are said to have built themselves a sort of hut or den adjoining the leper hospital. There they talked to each other, in the intervals of drudgery and danger (for it needed ten times more courage to look after a leper than to fight for the crown of Sicily), in the terms of their new life, almost like children talking a secret language. Of these individual elements on their first friendship we can say little with certainty; but it is certain that they remained friends to the end. Bernard of Quintavalle occupies in the story something of the position of Sir Bedivere, " first made and latest left of Arthur's knights," for he reappears again at the right hand of the saint on his death-bed and receives some sort of special blessing.

But all those things belong to another historical world and were quite remote from the ragged and fantastic trio in their tumble-down hut. They were not monks except perhaps in the most literal and archaic sense which was identical with hermits. They were, so to speak, three solitaries living together socially, but not as a society. The whole thing seems to have been intensely individual, as seen from the outside doubtless individual to the point of insanity. The stir of something that had in it the promise of a movement or a mission can first be felt as I have said in the affair of the appeal to the New Testament.

It was a sort of *sors virgiliana* applied to the Bible; a practice not unknown among Protestants though open to their criticism, one would think, as being rather a superstition of pagans. Anyhow it seems almost the opposite of searching the Scriptures to open them at random; but St. Francis certainly opened them at random. According to one story, he merely made the sign of the cross over the volume of the Gospel and opened it at three places reading three texts. The first was the tale of the rich young man whose refusal to sell all his goods was the occasion of the great paradox about the camel and the needle. The second was the commandment to the disciples to take nothing with them on their journey, neither scrip nor staff nor any money.

The third was that saying, literally to be called crucial, that the follower of Christ must also carry his cross There is a somewhat similar story of Francis finding one of these texts, almost as accidentally, merely in listening to what happened to be the Gospel of the day. But from the former version at least it would seem that the incident occurred very early indeed in his new life, perhaps soon after his breach with his father; for it was after this oracle, apparently, that Bernard the first disciple rushed forth and scattered all his goods among the poor. If this be so, it would seem that nothing followed it for the moment except the individual ascetical life with the hut for a hermitage. It must of course have been a rather public sort of hermitage, but it was none the less in a very real sense withdrawn from the world. St. Simeon Stylites on the top of his pillar was in one sense an exceedingly public character; but there was something a little singular in his situation for all that. It may be presumed that most people thought the situation of Francis singular, that some even thought it too singular. There was inevitably indeed in any Catholic society something ultimate and even subconscious that was at least capable of comprehending it better than a pagan or puritan society could comprehend it. But we must not at this stage, I think, exaggerate this potential public sympathy. As has already been suggested, the Church and all its institutions had already the air of being old and settled and sensible things, the monastic institutions among the rest. Common sense was commoner in the Middle Ages, I think, than in our own rather jumpy journalistic age; but men like Francis are not common in any age, nor are they to be fully understood merely by the exercise of common sense. The thirteenth century was certainly a progressive period; perhaps the only really progressive period in human history. But it can truly be called progressive precisely because its progress was very orderly. It is really and truly an example of an epoch of reforms without revolutions. But the reforms were not only progressive but very practical; and they were very much to the advantage of highly practical institutions; the towns and the trading guilds and the manual crafts. Now the solid men of town and guild in the time of Francis of Assisi were probably very solid indeed. They were much more economically equal, they were much more justly governed in their own economic environment, than the moderns who struggle madly between starvation and the monopolist prizes of capitalism; but it is likely enough that the majority of such citizens were as hard-headed as peasants. Certainly the behaviour of the venerable Peter Bernardone does not indicate a delicate sympathy

with the fine and almost fanciful subtleties of
the Franciscan spirit. And we cannot measure
the beauty and originality of this strange spiritual
adventure, unless we have the humour and
human sympathy to put into plain words how
it would have looked to such an unsympathetic
person at the time when it happened. In the
next chapter I shall make an attempt, inevitably inadequate, to indicate the inside of this
story of the building of the three churches and
the little hut. In this chapter I have but out-
lined it from the outside. And in concluding
that chapter I ask the reader to remember and
realise what that story really looked like, when
thus seen from the outside. Given a critic
of rather coarse common sense, with no feeling
about the incident except annoyance, and how
would the story seem to stand?

A young fool or rascal is caught robbing his
father and selling goods which he ought to
guard; and the only explanation he will offer
is that a loud voice from nowhere spoke in his
ear and told him to mend the cracks and holes
in a particular wall. He then declares himself
naturally independent of all powers corresponding
to the police or the magistrates, and takes refuge
with an amiable bishop who is forced to remon-
strate with him and tell him he is wrong. He
then proceeds to take off his clothes in public
and practically throw them at his father;

announcing at the same time that his father is not his father at all. He then runs about the town asking everybody he meets to give him fragments of buildings or building materials, apparently with reference to his old monomania about mending the wall. It may be an excellent thing that cracks should be filled up, but preferably not by somebody who is himself cracked; and architectural restoration like other things is not best performed by builders who, as we should say, have a tile loose. Finally the wretched youth relapses into rags and squalor and practically crawls away into the gutter. That is the spectacle that Francis must have presented to a very large number of his neighbours and friends.

How he lived at all must have seemed to them dubious; but presumably he already begged for bread as he had begged for building materials. But he was always very careful to beg for the blackest or worst bread he could get, for the stalest crusts or something rather less luxurious than the crumbs which the dogs eat, and which fall from the rich man's table. Thus he probably fared worse than an ordinary beggar; for the beggar would eat the best he could get and the saint ate the worst he could get. In plain fact he was ready to live on refuse; and it was probably something much uglier as an experience than the refined simplicity which vegetarians and water-drinkers would call the simple life. As he dealt

with the question of food, so he apparently
dealt with the question of clothing. He dealt
with it, that is, upon the same principle of taking
what he could get, and not even the best of what
he could get. According to one story he changed
clothes with a beggar; and he would doubtless
have been content to change them with a scare-
crow. In another version he got hold of the
rough brown tunic of a peasant, but presumably
only because the peasant gave him his very
oldest brown tunic, which was probably very
old indeed. Most peasants have few changes of
clothing to give away; and some peasants are
not specially inclined to give them away until it
is absolutely necessary. It is said that in place
of the girdle which he had flung off (perhaps with
the more symbolic scorn because it probably
carried the purse or wallet by the fashion of the
period) he picked up a rope more or less at random,
because it was lying near, and tied it round his
waist. He undoubtedly meant it as a shabby
expedient; rather as the very destitute tramp
will sometimes tie his clothes together with a
piece of string. He meant to strike the note
of collecting his clothes anyhow, like rags from
a succession of dust-bins. Ten years later that
make-shift costume was the uniform of five
thousand men; and a hundred years later, in
that, for a pontifical panoply, they laid great
Dante in the grave.

MANY signs and symbols might be used to give a hint of what really happened in the mind of the young poet of Assisi. Indeed they are at once too numerous for selection and yet too slight for satisfaction. But one of them may be adumbrated in this small and apparently accidental fact: that when he and his secular companions carried their pageant of poetry through the town, they called themselves Troubadours. But when he and his spiritual companions came out to do their spiritual work in the world, they were called by their leader the Jongleurs de Dieu.

Nothing has been said here at any length of the great culture of the Troubadours as it appeared in Provence or Languedoc, great as was their influence in history and their influence on St. Francis. Something more may be said of them when we come to summarise his relation to history; it is enough to note here in a few sentences the facts about them that were relevant to him, and especially the particular point now in question, which was the most relevant of all. Everybody knows who the Troubadours were; everybody knows that very early in the Middle Ages, in the twelfth and early thirteenth centuries, there arose a civilisation in Southern France which threatened to rival or eclipse the rising tradition of Paris. Its chief product was a school of poetry, or rather more especially a school of poets. They were primarily love-poets, though they were often also satirists and critics of things in general. Their picturesque posture in history is largely due to the fact that they sang their own poems and often played their own accompaniments, on the light musical instruments of the period; they were minstrels as well as men of letters. Allied to their love-poetry were other institutions of a decorative and fanciful kind concerned with the same theme. There was what was called the " Gay Science," the attempt to reduce to a sort of system the fine shades of flirtation and philandering. There were the things called Courts of Love, in which the same delicate subjects were dealt with with legal pomp and pedantry. There is one point in this part of the business that must be remembered in relation to St. Francis. There were manifest moral dangers in all this superb sentimentalism; but it is a mistake to suppose that its only danger of exaggeration was in the direction of sensualism. There was a strain in the southern romance that was actually an excess of spirituality; just as the pessimist heresy it produced was in one sense an excess of spirituality. The love was not always animal; sometimes it was so airy as to be almost allegorical. The reader realises that the lady is the most beautiful being that can possibly exist, only he has occasional doubts as to whether she does exist. Dante owed something to the Troubadours; and the critical debates about his ideal woman are an excellent example of these doubts. We know that Beatrice was not his wife, but we should in any case be equally sure that she was not his mistress; and some critics have even suggested that she was nothing at all, so to speak, except his muse. This idea of Beatrice as an allegorical figure is, I believe, unsound; it would seem unsound to any man who has read the *Vita Nuova* and has been in love. But the very fact that it is possible to suggest it illustrates something abstract and scholastic in these medieval passions. But though they were abstract passions they were very passionate passions. These men could feel almost like lovers, even about allegories and abstractions. It is necessary to remember this in order to realise that St. Francis was talking the true language of a troubadour when he said that he also had a most glorious and gracious lady and that her name was Poverty.

But the particular point to be noted here is not concerned so much with the word Troubadour

as with the word Jongleur. It is especially concerned with the transition from one to the other;
and for this it is necessary to grasp another detail
about the poets of the Gay Science. A jongleur
was not the same thing as a troubadour, even if
the same man were both a troubadour and a
jongleur. More often, I believe, they were separate
men as well as separate trades. In many cases
apparently the two men would walk the world
together like companions in arms, or rather
companions in arts. The jongleur was properly
a joculator or jester; sometimes he was what we
should call a juggler. This is the point, I imagine,
of the tale about Taillefer the Jongleur at the
battle of Hastings, who sang of the death of Roland
while he tossed up his sword and caught it, as a
juggler catches balls. Sometimes he may have
been even a tumbler; like that acrobat in the
beautiful legend who was called " The Tumbler of
Our Lady," because he turned head over heels and
stood on his head before the image of the Blessed
Virgin, for which he was nobly thanked and
comforted by her and the whole company of
heaven. In the ordinary way, we may imagine,
the troubadour would exalt the company with
earnest and solemn strains of love and then the
jongleur would do his turn as a sort of comic
relief. A glorious medieval romance remains to
be written about two such companions wandering
through the world. At any rate, if there is one

place in which the true Franciscan spirit can be found outside the true Franciscan story, it is in that tale of the Tumbler of Our Lady. And when St. Francis called his followers the Jongleurs de Dieu, he meant something very like the Tumblers of Our Lord.

Somewhere in that transition from the ambition of the Troubadour to the antics of the Tumbler is hidden, as under a parable, the truth of St. Francis. Of the two minstrels or entertainers, the jester was presumably the servant or at least the secondary figure. St. Francis really meant what he said when he said he had found the secret of life in being the servant and the secondary figure. There was to be found ultimately in such service a freedom almost amounting to frivolity. It was comparable to the condition of the jongleur because it almost amounted to frivolity. The jester could be free when the knight was rigid; and it was possible to be a jester in the service which is perfect freedom. This parallel of the two poets or minstrels is perhaps the best preliminary and external statement of the Franciscan change of heart, being conceived under an image with which the imagination of the modern world has a certain sympathy. There was, of course, a great deal more than this involved; and we must endeavour however insufficiently to penetrate past the image to the idea. It is so far like the tumblers that it is really to many people a topsy-turvy idea.

Francis, at the time or somewhere about the time when he disappeared into the prison or the dark cavern, underwent a reversal of a certain psychological kind; which was really like the reversal of a complete somersault, in that by coming full circle it came back, or apparently came back, to the same normal posture. It is necessary to use the grotesque simile of an acrobatic antic, because there is hardly any other figure that will make the fact clear. But in the inward sense it was a profound spiritual revolution. The man who went into the cave was not the man who came out again; in that sense he was almost as different as if he were dead, as if he were a ghost or a blessed spirit. And the effects of this on his attitude towards the actual world were really as extravagant as any parallel can make them. He looked at the world as differently from other men as if he had come out of that dark hole walking on his hands.

If we apply this parable of Our Lady's Tumbler to the case, we shall come very near to the point of it. Now it really is a fact that any scene such as a landscape can sometimes be more clearly and freshly seen if it is seen upside down. There have been landscape-painters who adopted the most startling and pantomimic postures in order to look at it for a moment in that fashion. Thus that inverted vision, so much more bright and quaint and arresting, does bear a certain resemblance to the world which a mystic like St. Francis sees every day. But herein is the essential part of the parable. Our Lady's Tumbler did not stand on his head *in order* to see flowers and trees as a clearer or quainter vision. He did not do so; and it would never have occurred to him to do so. Our Lady's Tumbler stood on his head to please Our Lady. If St. Francis had done the same thing, as he was quite capable of doing, it would originally have been from the same motive; a motive of a purely supernatural thought. It would be *after* this that his enthusiasm would extend itself and give a sort of halo to the edges of all earthly things. This is why it is not true to represent St. Francis as a mere romantic forerunner of the Renaissance and a revival of natural pleasures for their own sake. The whole point of him was that the secret of recovering the natural pleasures lay in regarding them in the light of a supernatural pleasure. In other words, he repeated in his own person that historic process noted in the introductory chapter; the vigil of asceticism which ends in the vision of a natural world made new. But in the personal case there was even more than this; there were elements that make the parallel of the Jongleur or Tumbler even more appropriate than this.

It may be suspected that in that black cell or cave Francis passed the blackest hours of his life. By nature he was the sort of man who has that vanity which is the opposite of pride; that vanity which is very near to humility. He never despised his fellow creatures and therefore he never despised the opinion of his fellow creatures; including the admiration of his fellow creatures. All that part of his human nature had suffered the heaviest and most crushing blows. It is possible that after his humiliating return from his frustrated military campaign he was called a coward. It is certain that after his quarrel with his father about the bales of cloth he was called a thief. And even those who had sympathised most with him, the priest whose church he had restored, the bishop whose blessing he had received, had evidently treated him with an almost humorous amiability which left only too clear the ultimate conclusion of the matter. He had made a fool of himself. Any man who has been young, who has ridden horses or thought himself ready for a fight, who has fancied himself as a troubadour and accepted the conventions of comradeship, will appreciate the ponderous and crushing weight of that simple phrase. The conversion of St. Francis, like the conversion of St. Paul, involved his being in some sense flung suddenly from a horse; but in a sense it was an even worse fall; for it was a war-horse. Anyhow, there was not a rag of him left that was not ridiculous. Everybody knew that at the best he had made a fool of himself. It was a solid objective fact, like the stones in the road,

F

that he had made a fool of himself. He saw himself as an object, very small and distinct like a fly walking on a clear window pane; and it was unmistakably a fool. And as he stared at the word " fool " written in luminous letters before him, the word itself began to shine and change.

We used to be told in the nursery that if a man were to bore a hole through the centre of the earth and climb continually down and down, there would come a moment at the centre when he would seem to be climbing up and up. I do not know whether this is true. The reason I do not know whether it is true is that I never happened to bore a hole through the centre of the earth, still less to crawl through it. If I do not know what this reversal or inversion feels like, it is because I have never been there. And this also is an allegory. It is certain that the writer, it is even possible that the reader, is an ordinary person who has never been there. We cannot follow St Francis to that final spiritual overturn in which complete humiliation becomes complete holiness or happiness, because we have never been there. I for one do not profess to follow it any further than that first breaking down of the romantic barricades of boyish vanity, which I have suggested in the last paragraph. And even that paragraph, of course, is merely conjectural, an individual guess at what he may have felt; but he may have felt something quite different. But

whatever else it was, it was so far analogous to
the story of the man making a tunnel through the
earth that it did mean a man going down and
down until at some mysterious moment he begins
to go up and up. We have never gone up like
that because we have never gone down like that;
we are obviously incapable of saying that it does
not happen; and the more candidly and calmly
we read human history, and especially the history
of the wisest men, the more we shall come to the
conclusion that it does happen. Of the intrinsic
internal essence of the experience I make no
pretence of writing at all. But the external effect
of it, for the purpose of this narrative, may be
expressed by saying that when Francis came forth
from his cave of vision, he was wearing the same
word " fool " as a feather in his cap; as a crest
or even a crown. He would go on being a fool;
he would become more and more of a fool; he
would be the court fool of the King of Paradise.

This state can only be represented in symbol;
but the symbol of inversion is true in another way.
If a man saw the world upside down, with all the
trees and towers hanging head downwards as in
a pool, one effect would be to emphasise the idea
of *dependence*. There is a Latin and literal connection; for the very word dependence only means
hanging. It would make vivid the Scriptural
text which says that God has hanged the world
upon nothing. If St. Francis had seen, in one of

his strange dreams, the town of Assisi upside down, it need not have differed in a single detail from itself except in being entirely the other way round. But the point is this : that whereas to the normal eye the large masonry of its walls or the massive foundations of its watchtowers and its high citadel would make it seem safer and more permanent, the moment it was turned over the very same weight would make it seem more helpless and more in peril. It is but a symbol; but it happens to fit the psychological fact. St. Francis might love his little town as much as before, or more than before; but the nature of the love would be altered even in being increased. He might see and love every tile on the steep roofs or every bird on the battlements; but he would see them all in a new and divine light of eternal danger and dependence. Instead of being merely proud of his strong city because it could not be moved, he would be thankful to God Almighty that it had not been dropped; he would be thankful to God for not dropping the whole cosmos like a vast crystal to be shattered into falling stars. Perhaps St. Peter saw the world so, when he was crucified head-downwards.

It is commonly in a somewhat cynical sense that men have said, " Blessed is he that expecteth nothing, for he shall not be disappointed." It was in a wholly happy and enthusiastic sense that St. Francis said, " Blessed is he who expecteth

nothing, for he shall enjoy everything." It was
by this deliberate idea of starting from zero, from
the dark nothingness of his own deserts, that he
did come to enjoy even earthly things as few
people have enjoyed them; and they are in themselves the best working example of the idea. For
there is no way in which a man can earn a star or
deserve a sunset. But there is more than this
involved, and more indeed than is easily to be
expressed in words. It is not only true that the
less a man thinks of himself, the more he thinks
of his good luck and of all the gifts of God. It is
also true that he sees more of the things themselves
when he sees more of their origin; for their origin
is a part of them and indeed the most important
part of them. Thus they become more extraordinary by being explained. He has more wonder
at them but less fear of them; for a thing is
really wonderful when it is significant and not
when it is insignificant; and a monster, shapeless
or dumb or merely destructive, may be larger
than the mountains, but is still in a literal sense
insignificant. For a mystic like St. Francis the
monsters had a meaning; that is, they had
delivered their message. They spoke no longer
in an unknown tongue. That is the meaning
of all those stories, whether legendary or historical, in which he appears as a magician
speaking the language of beasts and birds.
The mystic will have nothing to do with mere

mystery; mere mystery is generally a mystery of iniquity.

The transition from the good man to the saint is a sort of revolution; by which one for whom all things illustrate and illuminate God becomes one for whom God illustrates and illuminates all things. It is rather like the reversal whereby a lover might say at first sight that a lady looked like a flower, and say afterwards that all flowers reminded him of his lady. A saint and a poet standing by the same flower might seem to say the same thing; but indeed though they would both be telling the truth, they would be telling different truths. For one the joy of life is a cause of faith, for the other rather a result of faith. But one effect of the difference is that the sense of a divine dependence, which for the artist is like the brilliant levin-blaze, for the saint is like the broad daylight. Being in some mystical sense on the other side of things, he sees things go forth from the divine as children going forth from a familiar and accepted home, instead of meeting them as they come out, as most of us do, upon the roads of the world. And it is the paradox that by this privilege he is more familiar, more free and fraternal, more carelessly hospitable than we. For us the elements are like heralds who tell us with trumpet and tabard that we are drawing near the city of a great king; but he hails them with an old familiarity that is almost an old frivolity. He calls them his Brother Fire and his Sister Water.

So arises out of this almost nihilistic abyss the noble thing that is called Praise; which no one will ever understand while he identifies it with nature-worship or pantheistic optimism. When we say that a poet praises the whole creation, we commonly mean only that he praises the whole cosmos. But this sort of poet does really praise creation, in the sense of the act of creation. He praises the passage or transition from nonentity to entity; there falls here also the shadow of that archetypal image of the bridge, which has given to the priest his archaic and mysterious name. The mystic who passes through the moment when there is nothing but God does in some sense behold the beginningless beginnings in which there was really nothing else. He not only appreciates everything but the nothing of which everything was made. In a fashion he endures and answers even the earthquake irony of the Book of Job; in some sense he is there when the foundations of the world are laid, with the morning stars singing together and the sons of God shouting for joy. That is but a distant adumbration of the reason why the Franciscan, ragged, penniless, homeless and apparently hopeless, did indeed come forth singing such songs as might come from the stars of morning; and shouting, a son of God.

This sense of the great gratitude and the sublime

dependence was not a phrase or even a sentiment; it is the whole point that this was the very rock of reality. It was not a fancy but a fact; rather it is true that beside it all facts are fancies. That we all depend in every detail, at every instant, as a Christian would say upon God, as even an agnostic would say upon existence and the nature of things, is not an illusion of imagination; on the contrary, it is the fundamental fact which we cover up, as with curtains, with the illusion of ordinary life. That ordinary life is an admirable thing in itself, just as imagination is an admirable thing in itself. But it is much more the ordinary life that is made of imagination than the contemplative life. He who has seen the whole world hanging on a hair of the mercy of God has seen the truth; we might almost say the cold truth. He who has seen the vision of his city upside-down has seen it the right way up.

Rossetti makes the remark somewhere, bitterly but with great truth, that the worst moment for the atheist is when he is really thankful and has nobody to thank. The converse of this proposition is also true; and it is certain that this gratitude produced, in such men as we are here considering, the most purely joyful moments that have been known to man. The great painter boasted that he mixed all his colours with brains, and the great saint may be said to mix all his thoughts with thanks. All goods look better when they look like gifts. In this sense it is certain that the mystical method establishes a very healthy external relation to everything else. But it must always be remembered that everything else has for ever fallen into a second place, in comparison with this simple fact of dependence on the divine reality. In so far as ordinary social relations have in them something that seems solid and self-supporting, some sense of being at once buttressed and cushioned; in so far as they establish sanity in the sense of security and security in the sense of self-sufficiency, the man who has seen the world hanging on a hair does have some difficulty in taking them so seriously as that. In so far as even the secular authorities and hierarchies, even the most natural superiorities and the most necessary subordinations, tend at once to put a man in his place, and to make him sure of his position, the man who has seen the human hierarchy upside down will always have something of a smile for its superiorities. In this sense the direct vision of divine reality does disturb solemnities that are sane enough in themselves. The mystic may have added a cubit to his stature; but he generally loses something of his status. He can no longer take himself for granted, merely because he can verify his own existence in a parish register or a family Bible. Such a man may have something of the appearance of the lunatic who has lost his name while preserving his nature; who straightway forgets what manner of man he was. " Hitherto I have called Pietro Bernardone father; but now I am the servant of God."

All these profound matters must be suggested in short and imperfect phrases; and the shortest statement of one aspect of this illumination is to say that it is the discovery of an infinite debt. It may seem a paradox to say that a man may be transported with joy to discover that he is in debt. But this is only because in commercial cases the creditor does not generally share the transports of joy; especially when the debt is by hypothesis infinite and therefore unrecoverable. But here again the parallel of a natural love-story of the nobler sort disposes of the difficulty in a flash. There the infinite creditor does share the joy of the infinite debtor; for indeed they are both debtors and both creditors. In other words debt and dependence do become pleasures in the presence of unspoilt love; the word is used too loosely and luxuriously in popular simplifications like the present; but here the word is really the key. It is the key of all the problems of Franciscan morality which puzzle the merely modern mind; but above all it is the key of asceticism. It is the highest and holiest of the paradoxes that the man who really knows he cannot pay his debt will be for ever paying it. He will be for ever giving back what he cannot give back, and cannot be expected to give back. He will be always throwing things away into a bottomless pit of unfathomable thanks. Men who think they are too modern to understand this are in fact too mean to understand it; we are most of us too mean to practise it. We are not generous enough to be ascetics; one might almost say not genial enough to be ascetics. A man must have magnanimity of surrender, of which he commonly only catches a glimpse in first love, like a glimpse of our lost Eden. But whether he sees it or not, the truth is in that riddle; that the whole world has, or is, only one good thing; and it is a bad debt.

If ever that rarer sort of romantic love, which was the truth that sustained the Troubadours, falls out of fashion and is treated as fiction, we may see some such misunderstanding as that of the modern world about asceticism. For it seems conceivable that some barbarians might try to destroy chivalry in love, as the barbarians ruling in Berlin destroyed chivalry in war. If that were ever so, we should have the same sort of unintelligent sneers and unimaginative questions. Men will ask what selfish sort of woman it must have been who ruthlessly exacted tribute in the form of flowers, or what an avaricious creature she can have been to demand solid gold in the form of a ring; just as they ask what cruel kind of God can have demanded sacrifice and self-denial. They will have lost the clue to all that lovers have meant

by love; and will not understand that it was
because the thing was not demanded that it was
done. But whether or no any such lesser things
will throw a light on the greater, it is utterly
useless to study a great thing like the Franciscan
movement while remaining in the modern mood
that murmurs against gloomy asceticism. The
whole point about St. Francis of Assisi is that he
certainly was ascetical and he certainly was not
gloomy. As soon as ever he had been unhorsed
by the glorious humiliation of his vision of dependence on the divine love, he flung himself
into fasting and vigil exactly as he had flung
himself furiously into battle. He had wheeled
his charger clean round, but there was no halt
or check in the thundering impetuosity of his
charge. There was nothing negative about it; it
was not a regimen or a stoical simplicity of life.
It was not self-denial merely in the sense of self-
control. It was as positive as a passion; it had
all the air of being as positive as a pleasure. He
devoured fasting as a man devours food. He
plunged after poverty as men have dug madly for
gold. And it is precisely the positive and passionate quality of this part of his personality that is
a challenge to the modern mind in the whole problem of the pursuit of pleasure. There undeniably
is the historical fact; and there attached to it is
another moral fact almost as undeniable. It is
certain that he held on this heroic or unnatural

course from the moment when he went forth in his hair-shirt into the winter woods to the moment when he desired even in his death agony to lie bare upon the bare ground, to prove that he had and that he was nothing. And we can say, with almost as deep a certainty, that the stars which passed above that gaunt and wasted corpse stark upon the rocky floor had for once, in all their shining cycles round the world of labouring humanity, looked down upon a happy man.

FROM that cavern, that was a furnace of glowing gratitude and humility, there came forth one of the strongest and strangest and most original personalities that human history has known. He was, among other things, emphatically what we call a character; almost as we speak of a character in a good novel or play. He was not only a humanist but a humorist; a humorist especially in the old English sense of a man always in his humour, going his own way and doing what nobody else would have done. The anecdotes about him have a certain biographical quality of which the most familiar example is Dr. Johnson; which belongs in another way to William Blake or to Charles Lamb. The atmosphere can only be defined by a sort of antithesis; the act is always unexpected and never inappropriate. Before the thing is said or done it cannot even be conjectured; but after it is said or done it is felt to be merely characteristic. It is surprisingly and yet inevitably individual. This quality of abrupt fitness and bewildering consistency belongs to St. Francis in a way that marks him out from most men of his time. Men are learning more and more of the solid social virtues of medieval civilisation; but those impressions are still social rather than individual. The medieval world was far ahead of the modern world in its sense of the things in which all men are at one: death and the daylight of reason and the common conscience that holds communities together. Its generalisations were saner and sounder than the mad materialistic theories of to-day; nobody would have tolerated a Schopenhauer scorning life or a Nietzsche living only for scorn. But the modern world is more subtle in its sense of the things in which men are not at one; in the temperamental varieties and differentiations that make up the personal problems of life. All men who can think themselves now realise that the great schoolmen had a type of thought that was wonderfully clear; but it was as it were deliberately colourless. All are now agreed that the greatest art of the age was the art of public buildings; the popular and communal art of architecture. But it was not an age for the art of portrait-painting. Yet the friends of St. Francis have really contrived to leave behind a portrait; something almost resembling a devout and affectionate caricature. There are lines and colours in it that are personal almost to the extent of being perverse, if one can use the word perversity of an inversion that was also a conversion.

Even among the saints he has the air of a sort of eccentric, if one may use the word of one whose eccentricity consisted in always turning towards the centre.

Before resuming the narrative of his first adventures, and the building of the great brotherhood which was the beginning of so merciful a revolution, I think it well to complete this imperfect personal portrait here; and having attempted in the last chapter a tentative description of the process, to add in this chapter a few touches to describe the result. I mean by the result the real man as he was after his first formative experiences; the man whom men met walking about on the Italian roads in his brown tunic tied with a rope. For that man, saving the grace of God, is the explanation of all that followed; men acted quite differently according to whether they had met him or not. If we see afterwards a vast tumult, an appeal to the Pope, mobs of men in brown habits besieging the seats of authority, Papal pronouncements, heretical sessions, trial and triumphant survival, the world full of a new movement, the friar a household word in every corner of Europe, and if we ask *why* all this happened, we can only approximate to any answer to our own question if we can, in some faint and indirect imaginative fashion, hear one human voice or see one human face under a hood. There is no answer except that Francis Bernardone had happened; and we must try in some sense to see what we should have seen if he had happened to us. In other words, after some groping suggestions about his life from the inside, we must again consider it from the outside; as if he were a stranger coming up the road towards us, along the hills of Umbria, between the olives or the vines.

Francis of Assisi was slight in figure with that sort of slightness which, combined with so much vivacity, gives the impression of smallness. He was probably taller than he looked; middle-sized, his biographers say; he was certainly very active and, considering what he went through, must have been tolerably tough. He was of the brownish Southern colouring, with a dark beard thin and pointed such as appears in pictures under the hoods of elves; and his eyes glowed with the fire that fretted him night and day. There is something about the description of all he said and did which suggests that, even more than most Italians, he turned naturally to a passionate pantomime of gestures. If this was so it is equally certain that with him, even more than with most Italians, the gestures were all gestures of politeness or hospitality. And both these facts, the vivacity and the courtesy, are the outward signs of something that mark him out very distinctively from many who might appear to be more of his kind than they really are. It is truly said

G

that Francis of Assisi was one of the founders of
the medieval drama, and therefore of the modern
drama. He was the very reverse of a theatrical
person in the selfish sense; but for all that he was
pre-eminently a dramatic person. This side
of him can best be suggested by taking what is
commonly regarded as a reposeful quality; what
is commonly described as a love of nature. We
are compelled to use the term; and it is entirely
the wrong term.

St. Francis was not a lover of nature. Properly
understood, a lover of nature was precisely what
he was not. The phrase implies accepting the
material universe as a vague environment, a sort
of sentimental pantheism. In the romantic
period of literature, in the age of Byron and Scott,
it was easy enough to imagine that a hermit in
the ruins of a chapel (preferably by moonlight)
might find peace and a mild pleasure in the
harmony of solemn forests and silent stars, while
he pondered over some scroll or illuminated
volume, about the liturgical nature of which the
author was a little vague. In short, the hermit
might love nature as a background. Now for
St. Francis nothing was ever in the background.
We might say that his mind had no background,
except perhaps that divine darkness out of which
the divine love had called up every coloured
creature one by one. He saw everything as
dramatic, distinct from its setting, not all of a

piece like a picture but in action like a play. A bird went by him like an arrow; something with a story and a purpose, though it was a purpose of life and not a purpose of death. A bush could stop him like a brigand; and indeed he was as ready to welcome the brigand as the bush.

In a word, we talk about a man who cannot see the wood for the trees. St. Francis was a man who did not want to see the wood for the trees. He wanted to see each tree as a separate and almost a sacred thing, being a child of God and therefore a brother or sister of man. But he did not want to stand against a piece of stage scenery used merely as a background, and inscribed in a general fashion : " Scene; a wood." In this sense we might say that he was too dramatic for the drama. The scenery would have come to life in his comedies; the walls would really have spoken like Snout the Tinker and the trees would really have come walking to Dunsinane. Everything would have been in the foreground; and in that sense in the footlights. Everything would be in every sense a character. This is the quality in which, as a poet, he is the very opposite of a pantheist. He did not call nature his mother; he called a particular donkey his brother or a particular sparrow his sister. If he had called a pelican his aunt or an elephant his uncle, as he might possibly have done, he would still have meant that they were particular creatures assigned by their

Creator to particular places; not mere expressions of the evolutionary energy of things. That is where his mysticism is so close to the common sense of the child. A child has no difficulty about understanding that God made the dog and the cat; though he is well aware that the making of dogs and cats out of nothing is a mysterious process beyond his own imagination. But no child would understand what you meant if you mixed up the dog and the cat and everything else into one monster with a myriad legs and called it nature. The child would resolutely refuse to make head or tail of any such animal. St. Francis was a mystic, but he believed in mysticism and not in mystification. As a mystic he was the mortal enemy of all those mystics who melt away the edges of things and dissolve an entity into its environment. He was a mystic of the daylight and the darkness; but not a mystic of the twilight. He was the very contrary of that sort of oriental visionary who is only a mystic because he is too much of a sceptic to be a materialist. St. Francis was emphatically a realist, using the word realist in its much more real medieval sense. In this matter he really was akin to the best spirit of his age, which had just won its victory over the nominalism of the twelfth century. In this indeed there was something symbolic in the contemporary art and decoration of his period; as in the art of heraldry. The Franciscan birds and beasts were really rather like heraldic birds and beasts; not in the sense of being fabulous animals but in the sense of being treated as if they were facts, clear and positive and unaffected by the illusions of atmosphere and perspective. In that sense he did see a bird sable on a field azure or a sheep argent on a field vert. But the heraldry of humility was richer than the heraldry of pride; for it saw all these things that God had given as something more precious and unique than the blazonry that princes and peers had only given to themselves. Indeed out of the depths of that surrender it rose higher than the highest titles of the feudal age; than the laurel of Cæsar or the Iron Crown of Lombardy. It is an example of extremes that meet, that the Little Poor Man, who had stripped himself of everything and named himself as nothing, took the same title that has been the wild vaunt of the vanity of the gorgeous Asiatic autocrat, and called himself the Brother of the Sun and Moon.

This quality, of something outstanding and even startling in things as St. Francis saw them, is here important as illustrating a character in his own life. As he saw all things dramatically, so he himself was always dramatic. We have to assume throughout, needless to say, that he was a poet and can only be understood as a poet. But he had one poetic privilege denied to most poets In that respect indeed he might be called the one happy

poet among all the unhappy poets of the world.
He was a poet whose whole life was a poem. He
was not so much a minstrel merely singing his
own songs as a dramatist capable of acting the
whole of his own play. The things he said were
more imaginative than the things he wrote. The
things he did were more imaginative than the
things he said. His whole course through life
was a series of scenes in which he had a sort of
perpetual luck in bringing things to a beautiful
crisis To talk about the art of living has come
to sound rather artificial than artistic. But St.
Francis did in a definite sense make the very act
of living an art, though it was an unpremeditated
art. Many of his acts will seem grotesque and
puzzling to a rationalistic taste. But they were
always acts and not explanations; and they
always meant what he meant them to mean. The
amazing vividness with which he stamped himself
on the memory and imagination of mankind is
very largely due to the fact that he was seen again
and again under such dramatic conditions. From
the moment when he rent his robes and flung them
at his father's feet to the moment when he
stretched himself in death on the bare earth in the
pattern of the cross, his life was made up of these
unconscious attitudes and unhesitating gestures.
It would be easy to fill page after page with
examples; but I will here pursue the method found
convenient everywhere in this short sketch, and

take one typical example, dwelling on it with a little more detail than would be possible in a catalogue, in the hope of making the meaning more clear. The example taken here occurred in the last days of his life, but it refers back in a rather curious fashion to the first; and rounds off the remarkable unity of that romance of religion.

The phrase about his brotherhood with the sun and moon, and with the water and the fire, occurs of course in his famous poem called the Canticle of the Creatures or the Canticle of the Sun. He sang it wandering in the meadows in the sunnier season of his own career, when he was pouring upwards into the sky all the passions of a poet. It is a supremely characteristic work, and much of St. Francis could be reconstructed from that work alone. Though in some ways the thing is as simple and straightforward as a ballad, there is a delicate instinct of differentiation in it. Notice, for instance, the sense of sex in inanimate things, which goes far beyond the arbitrary genders of a grammar It was not for nothing that he called fire his brother, fierce and gay and strong, and water his sister, pure and clear and inviolate. Remember that St Francis was neither encumbered nor assisted by all that Greek and Roman polytheism turned into allegory, which has been to European poetry often an inspiration, too often a convention. Whether he gained or lost by his contempt of learning, it never occurred to him

to connect Neptune and the nymphs with the
water or Vulcan and the Cyclops with the flame.
This point exactly illustrates what has already
been suggested; that, so far from being a revival
of paganism, the Franciscan renascence was a sort
of fresh start and first awakening after a forget-
fulness of paganism. Certainly it is responsible
for a certain freshness in the thing itself. Anyhow
St Francis was, as it were, the founder of a new
folk-lore; but he could distinguish his mermaids
from his mermen and his witches from his wizards.
In short, he had to make his own mythology; but
he knew at a glance the goddesses from the gods.
This fanciful instinct for the sexes is not the only
example of an imaginative instinct of the kind.
There is just the same quaint felicity in the fact
that he singles out the sun with a slightly more
courtly title besides that of brother; a phrase that
one king might use of another, corresponding to
" Monsieur notre frère." It is like a faint half
ironic shadow of the shining primacy that it had
held in the pagan heavens. A bishop is said to
have complained of a Nonconformist saying Paul
instead of Saint Paul; and to have added " He
might at least have called him Mr. Paul." So
St. Francis is free of all obligation to cry out in
praise or terror on the Lord God Apollo, but in
his new nursery heavens, he salutes him as Mr.
Sun. Those are the things in which he has a sort
of inspired infancy, only to be paralleled in nursery

tales Something of the same hazy but healthy
awe makes the story of Brer Fox and Brer Rabbit
refer respectfully to Mr. Man.

This poem, full of the mirth of youth and the
memories of childhood, runs through his whole
life like a refrain, and scraps of it turn up continually in the ordinary habit of his talk. Perhaps
the last appearance of its special language was in
an incident that has always seemed to me intensely
impressive, and is at any rate very illustrative of
the great manner and gesture of which I speak.
Impressions of that kind are a matter of imagination and in that sense of taste.   It is idle to argue
about them; for it is the whole point of them
that they have passed beyond words; and even
when they use words, seem to be completed by some
ritual movement like a blessing or a blow.   So, in a
supreme example, there is something far past all
exposition, something like the sweeping movement and mighty shadow of a hand, darkening
even the darkness of Gethsemane; "Sleep on
now, and take your rest. . . ." Yet there are
people who have started to paraphrase and
expand the story of the Passion.

St. Francis was a dying man. We might say
he was an old man, at the time this typical incident
occurred; but in fact he was only prematurely
old; for he was not fifty when he died, worn out
with his fighting and fasting life. But when he
came down from the awful asceticism and more

awful revelation of Alverno, he was a broken man. As will be apparent when these events are touched on in their turn, it was not only sickness and bodily decay that may well have darkened his life; he had been recently disappointed in his main mission to end the Crusades by the conversion of Islam; he had been still more disappointed by the signs of compromise and a more political or practical spirit in his own order; he had spent his last energies in protest. At this point he was told that he was going blind. If the faintest hint has been given here of what St Francis felt about the glory and pageantry of earth and sky, about the heraldic shape and colour and symbolism of birds and beasts and flowers, some notion may be formed of what it meant to him to go blind. Yet the remedy might well have seemed worse than the disease. The remedy, admittedly an uncertain remedy, was to cauterise the eye, and that without any anæsthetic In other words it was to burn his living eyeballs with a red-hot iron. Many of the tortures of martyrdom, which he envied in martyrology and sought vainly in Syria, can have been no worse. When they took the brand from the furnace, he rose as with an urbane gesture and spoke as to an invisible presence: " Brother Fire, God made you beautiful and strong and useful; I pray you be courteous with me."

If there be any such thing as the art of life, it seems to me that such a moment was one of its masterpieces. Not to many poets has it been given to remember their own poetry at such a moment, still less to live one of their own poems. Even William Blake would have been disconcerted if, while he was re-reading the noble lines " Tiger, tiger, burning bright," a real large live Bengal tiger had put his head in at the window of the cottage in Felpham, evidently with every intention of biting his head off. He might have wavered before politely saluting it, above all by calmly completing the recitation of the poem to the quadruped to whom it was dedicated. Shelley, when he wished to be a cloud or a leaf carried before the wind, might have been mildly surprised to find himself turning slowly head over heels in mid air a thousand feet above the sea. Even Keats, knowing that his hold on life was a frail one, might have been disturbed to discover that the true, the blushful Hippocrene of which he had just partaken freely had indeed contained a drug, which really ensured that he should cease upon the midnight with no pain. For Francis there was no drug; and for Francis there was plenty of pain. But his first thought was one of his first fancies from the songs of his youth. He remembered the time when a flame was a flower, only the most glorious and gaily coloured of the flowers in the garden of God; and when that shining thing returned to him in the shape of an instrument of torture, he hailed it from afar like an old friend, calling it by the nickname which might most truly be called its Christian name.

That is only one incident out of a life of such incidents; and I have selected it partly because it shows what is meant here by that shadow of gesture there is in all his words, the dramatic gesture of the south; and partly because its special reference to courtesy covers the next fact to be noted. The popular instinct of St. Francis, and his perpetual preoccupation with the idea of brotherhood, will be entirely misunderstood if it is understood in the sense of what is often called camaraderie; the back-slapping sort of brotherhood. Frequently from the enemies and too frequently from the friends of the democratic ideal, there has come a notion that this note is necessary to that ideal. It is assumed that equality means all men being equally uncivil, whereas it obviously ought to mean all men being equally civil Such people have forgotten the very meaning and derivation of the word civility, if they do not see that to be uncivil is to be uncivic. But anyhow that was not the equality which Francis of Assisi encouraged; but an equality of the opposite kind; it was a camaraderie actually founded on courtesy.

Even in that fairy borderland of his mere fancies about flowers and animals and even inanimate things, he retained this permanent posture of a sort of deference. A friend of mine said that somebody was the sort of man who apologises to the cat. St. Francis really would have apologised to the cat. When he was about to preach in a wood full of the chatter of birds, he said, with a gentle gesture " Little sisters, if you have now had your say, it is time that I also should be heard." And all the birds were silent; as I for one can very easily believe. In deference to my special design of making matters intelligible to average modernity, I have treated separately the subject of the miraculous powers that St Francis most certainly possessed But even apart from any miraculous powers, men of that magnetic sort, with that intense interest in animals, often have an extraordinary power over them. St. Francis's power was always exercised with this elaborate politeness. Much of it was doubtless a sort of symbolic joke, a pious pantomime intended to convey the vital distinction in his divine mission, that he not only loved but reverenced God in all his creatures. In this sense he had the air not only of apologising to the cat or to the birds, but of apologising to a chair for sitting on it or to a table for sitting down at it. Anyone who had followed him through life merely to laugh at him, as a sort of lovable lunatic, might easily have had an impression as of a lunatic who bowed to every post or took off his hat to every tree. This was all a part of his instinct for imaginative gesture. He taught the world a large part of

its lesson by a sort of divine dumb alphabet.   But
if there was this ceremonial element even in lighter
or lesser matters, its significance became far more
serious in the serious work of his life, which was
an appeal to humanity, or rather to human
beings.

I have said that St. Francis deliberately did
not see the wood for the trees.   It is even more
true that he deliberately did not see the mob for
the men.   What distinguishes this very genuine
democrat from any mere demagogue is that he
never either deceived or was deceived by the
illusion of mass-suggestion.   Whatever his taste
in monsters, he never saw before him a many-
headed beast.   He only saw the image of God
multiplied but never monotonous.   To him a man
was always a man and did not disappear in a dense
crowd any more than in a desert.   He honoured
all men; that is, he not only loved but respected
them all.   What gave him his extraordinary
personal power was this; that from the Pope to
the beggar, from the sultan of Syria in his
pavilion to the ragged robbers crawling out of the
wood, there was never a man who looked into
those brown burning eyes without being certain
that Francis Bernardone was really interested in
him ; in his own inner individual life from the
cradle to the grave; that he himself was being
valued and taken seriously, and not merely added
to the spoils of some social policy or the names in

some clerical document. Now for this particular
moral and religious idea there is no external
expression except courtesy. Exhortation does not
express it, for it is not mere abstract enthusiasm;
beneficence does not express it, for it is not mere
pity It can only be conveyed by a certain grand
manner which may be called good manners. We
may say if we like that St. Francis, in the bare
and barren simplicity of his life, had clung to one
rag of luxury; the manners of a court. But
whereas in a court there is one king and a hundred
courtiers, in this story there was one courtier,
moving among a hundred kings. For he treated
the whole mob of men as a mob of kings. And
this was really and truly the only attitude that
will appeal to that part of man to which he wished
to appeal. It cannot be done by giving gold or
even bread; for it is a proverb that any reveller
may fling largesse in mere scorn. It cannot even
be done by giving time and attention; for
any number of philanthropists and benevolent
bureaucrats do such work with a scorn far more
cold and horrible in their hearts. No plans or
proposals or efficient rearrangements will give
back to a broken man his self-respect and sense
of speaking with an equal One gesture will do it.

With that gesture Francis of Assisi moved
among men; and it was soon found to have something in it of magic and to act, in a double sense,
like a charm. But it must always be conceived

as a completely natural gesture; for indeed it was almost a gesture of apology. He must be imagined as moving thus swiftly through the world with a sort of impetuous politeness; almost like the movement of a man who stumbles on one knee half in haste and half in obeisance. The eager face under the brown hood was that of a man always going somewhere, as if he followed as well as watched the flight of the birds. And this sense of motion is indeed the meaning of the whole revolution that he made; for the work that has now to be described was of the nature of an earthquake or a volcano, an explosion that drove outwards with dynamic energy the forces stored up by ten centuries in the monastic fortress or arsenal and scattered all its riches recklessly to the ends of the earth. In a better sense than the antithesis commonly conveys, it is true to say that what St. Benedict had stored St. Francis scattered; but in the world of spiritual things what had been stored into the barns like grain was scattered over the world as seed. The servants of God who had been a besieged garrison became a marching army; the ways of the world were filled as with thunder with the trampling of their feet and far ahead of that ever swelling host went a man singing; as simply he had sung that morning in the winter woods, where he walked alone.

THERE is undoubtedly a sense in which two is company and three is none; there is also another sense in which three is company and four is none, as is proved by the procession of historic and fictitious figures moving three deep, the famous trios like the Three Musketeers or the Three Soldiers of Kipling. But there is yet another and a different sense in which four is company and three is none; if we use the word company in the vaguer sense of a crowd or a mass. With the fourth man enters the shadow of a mob; the group is no longer one of three individuals only conceived individually. That shadow of the fourth man fell across the little hermitage of the Portiuncula when a man named Egidio, apparently a poor workman, was invited by St. Francis to enter. He mingled without difficulty with the merchant and the canon who had already become the companions of Francis; but with his coming an invisible line was crossed; for it must have been felt by this time that the growth of that small group had become potentially infinite, or at least that its outline had become permanently indefinite. It may have been in the time of that transition that Francis had another of his dreams full of voices; but now the voices were a clamour of the tongues of all nations, Frenchmen and Italians and English and Spanish and Germans, telling of the glory of God each in his own tongue; a new Pentecost and a happier Babel.

Before describing the first steps he took to regularise the growing group, it is well to have a rough grasp of what he conceived that group to be. He did not call his followers monks; and it is not clear, at this time at least, that he even thought of them as monks. He called them by a name which is generally rendered in English as the Friars Minor; but we shall be much closer to the atmosphere of his own mind if we render it almost literally as The Little Brothers. Presumably he was already resolved, indeed, that they should take the three vows of poverty, chastity and obedience which had always been the mark of a monk. But it would seem that he was not so much afraid of the idea of a monk as of the idea of an abbot. He was afraid that the great spiritual magistracies which had given even to their holiest possessors at least a sort of impersonal and corporate pride, would import an element of pomposity that would spoil his extremely and almost extravagantly simple version of the life of humility. But the supreme difference between his discipline and the discipline of the old monastic

system was concerned, of course, with the idea
that the monks were to become migratory and
almost nomadic instead of stationary. They were
to mingle with the world; and to this the more
old-fashioned monk would naturally reply by
asking how they were to mingle with the world
without becoming entangled with the world. It
was a much more real question than a loose reli-
giosity is likely to realise; but St. Francis had his
answer to it, of his own individual sort; and the
interest of the problem is in that highly individual
answer.

The good Bishop of Assisi expressed a sort of
horror at the hard life which the Little Brothers
lived at the Portiuncula, without comforts, without possessions, eating anything they could get
and sleeping anyhow on the ground. St. Francis
answered him with that curious and almost
stunning shrewdness which the unworldly can
sometimes wield like a club of stone. He said,
" If we had any possessions, we should need
weapons and laws to defend them." That
sentence is the clue to the whole policy that he
pursued. It rested upon a real piece of logic;
and about that he was never anything but logical.
He was ready to own himself wrong about anything else; but he was quite certain he was right
about this particular rule. He was only once seen
angry; and that was when there was talk of an
exception to the rule.

His argument was this: that the dedicated man might go anywhere among any kind of men, even the worst kind of men, so long as there was nothing by which they could hold him. If he had any ties or needs like ordinary men, he would become like ordinary men. St. Francis was the last man in the world to think any the worse of ordinary men for being ordinary. They had more affection and admiration from him than they are ever likely to have again. But for his own particular purpose of stirring up the world to a new spiritual enthusiasm, he saw with a logical clarity that was quite reverse of fanatical or sentimental, that friars must not become like ordinary men; that the salt must not lose its savour even to turn into human nature's daily food. And the difference between a friar and an ordinary man was really that a friar was freer than an ordinary man. It was necessary that he should be free from the cloister; but it was even more important that he should be free from the world. It is perfectly sound common sense to say that there is a sense in which the ordinary man cannot be free from the world; or rather ought not to be free from the world. The feudal world in particular was one labyrinthine system of dependence; but it was not only the feudal world that went to make up the medieval world nor the medieval world that went to make up the whole world; and the whole world is full of this fact.

Family life as much as feudal life is in its nature a system of dependence. Modern trade unions as much as medieval guilds are interdependent among themselves even in order to be independent of others. In medieval as in modern life, even where these limitations do exist for the sake of liberty, they have in them a considerable element of luck. They are partly the result of circumstances; sometimes the almost unavoidable result of circumstances. So the twelfth century had been the age of vows; and there was something of relative freedom in that feudal gesture of the vow; for no man asks vows from slaves any more than from spades. Still, in practice, a man rode to war in support of the ancient house of the Column or behind the Great Dog of the Stairway largely because he had been born in a certain city or countryside. But no man need obey little Francis in the old brown coat unless he chose. Even in his relations with his chosen leader he was in one sense relatively free, compared with the world around him. He was obedient but not dependent. And he was as free as the wind, he was almost wildly free, in his relation to that world around him. The world around him was, as has been noted, a network of feudal and family and other forms of dependence. The whole idea of St. Francis was that the Little Brothers should be like little fishes who could go freely in and out of that net. They could do so precisely because they were small fishes and in that sense even slippery fishes. There was nothing that the world could hold them by; for the world catches us mostly by the fringes of our garments, the futile externals of our lives. One of the Franciscans says later, " A monk should own nothing but his harp "; meaning, I suppose, that he should value nothing but his song, the song with which it was his business as a minstrel to serenade every castle and cottage, the song of the joy of the Creator in his creation and the beauty of the brotherhood of men. In imagining the life of this sort of visionary vagabond, we may already get a glimpse also of the practical side of that asceticism which puzzles those who think themselves practical. A man had to be thin to pass always through the bars and out of the cage; he had to travel light in order to ride so fast and so far. It was the whole calculation, so to speak, of that innocent cunning, that the world was to be outflanked and outwitted by him, and be embarrassed about what to do with him. You could not threaten to starve a man who was ever striving to fast. You could not ruin him and reduce him to beggary, for he was already a beggar. There was a very luke-warm satisfaction even in beating him with a stick, when he only indulged in little leaps and cries of joy because indignity was his only dignity. You could not put his head in a halter without the risk of putting it in a halo.

But one distinction between the old monks and the new friars counted especially in the matter of practicality and especially of promptitude. The old fraternities with their fixed habitations and enclosed existence had the limitations of ordinary householders. However simply they lived there must be a certain number of cells or a certain number of beds or at least a certain cubic space for a certain number of brothers; their numbers therefore depended on their land and building material. But since a man could become a Franciscan by merely promising to take his chance of eating berries in a lane or begging a crust from a kitchen, of sleeping under a hedge or sitting patiently on a doorstep, there was no economic reason why there should not be any number of such eccentric enthusiasts within any short period of time. It must also be remembered that the whole of this rapid development was full of a certain kind of democratic optimism that really was part of the personal character of St. Francis. His very asceticism was in one sense the height of optimism. He demanded a great deal of human nature not because he despised it but rather because he trusted it. He was expecting a very great deal from the extraordinary men who followed him; but he was also expecting a good deal from the ordinary men to whom he sent them. He asked the laity for food as confidently as he asked the fraternity for fasting. But he counted on the hospitality of humanity because he really did regard every house as the house of a friend. He really did love and honour ordinary men and ordinary things; indeed we may say that he only sent out the extraordinary men to encourage men to be ordinary.

This paradox may be more exactly stated or explained when we come to deal with the very interesting matter of the Third Order, which was designed to assist ordinary men to be ordinary with an extraordinary exultation. The point at issue at present is the audacity and simplicity of the Franciscan plan for quartering its spiritual soldiery upon the population; not by force but by persuasion, and even by the persuasion of impotence. It was an act of confidence and therefore a compliment. It was completely successful. It was an example of something that clung about St. Francis always; a kind of tact that looked like luck because it was as simple and direct as a thunderbolt. There are many examples in his private relations of this sort of tactless tact; this surprise effected by striking at the heart of the matter. It is said that a young friar was suffering from a sort of sulks between morbidity and humility, common enough in youth and hero-worship, in which he had got it into his head that his hero hated or despised him. We can imagine how tactfully social diplomatists would steer clear of scenes and excitements, how cautiously psychologists would watch and handle such delicate cases. Francis suddenly walked up to the young man, who was of course secretive and silent as the grave, and said, " Be not troubled in your thoughts for you are dear to me, and even among the number of those who are most dear. You know that you are worthy of my friendship and society; therefore come to me, in confidence, whensoever you will, and from friendship learn faith." Exactly as he spoke to that morbid boy he spoke to all mankind. He always went to the point; he always seemed at once more right and more simple than the person he was speaking to. He seemed at once to be laying open his guard and yet lunging at the heart. Something in this attitude disarmed the world as it has never been disarmed again. He was better than other men; he was a benefactor of other men; and yet he was not hated. The world came into church by a newer and nearer door; and by friendship it learnt faith.

It was while the little knot of people at the Portiuncula was still small enough to gather in a small room that St. Francis resolved on his first important and even sensational stroke. It is said that there were only twelve Franciscans in the whole world when he decided to march, as it were, on Rome and found a Franciscan order. It would seem that this appeal to remote headquarters was not generally regarded as necessary;

possibly something could have been done in a secondary way under the Bishop of Assisi and the local clergy. It would seem even more probable that people thought it somewhat unnecessary to trouble the supreme tribunal of Christendom about what a dozen chance men chose to call themselves. But Francis was obstinate and as it were blind on this point; and his brilliant blindness is exceedingly characteristic of him. A man satisfied with small things, or even in love with small things, he yet never felt quite as we do about the disproportion between small things and large. He never saw things to scale in our sense, but with a dizzy disproportion which makes the mind reel. Sometimes it seems merely out of drawing like a gaily coloured medieval map; and then again it seems to have escaped from everything like a short cut in the fourth dimension. He is said to have made a journey to interview the Emperor, throned among his armies under the eagle of the Holy Roman Empire, to intercede for the lives of certain little birds. He was quite capable of facing fifty emperors to intercede for one bird. He started out with two companions to convert the Mahomedan world. He started out with eleven companions to ask the Pope to make a new monastic world.

Innocent III., the great Pope, according to Bonaventura, was walking on the terrace of St. John Lateran, doubtless revolving the great political questions which troubled his reign, when there appeared abruptly before him a person in peasant costume whom he took to be some sort of shepherd. He appears to have got rid of the shepherd with all convenient speed; possibly he formed the opinion that the shepherd was mad. Anyhow he thought no more about it until, says the great Franciscan biographer, he dreamed that night a strange dream. He fancied that he saw the whole huge ancient temple of St. John Lateran, on whose high terraces he had walked so securely, leaning horribly and crooked against the sky as if all its domes and turrets were stooping before an earthquake. Then he looked again and saw that a human figure was holding it up like a living caryatid; and the figure was that of the ragged shepherd or peasant from whom he had turned away on the terrace. Whether this be a fact or a figure it is a very true figure of the abrupt simplicity with which Francis won the attention and the favour of Rome. His first friend seems to have been the Cardinal Giovanni di San Paolo who pleaded for the Franciscan idea before a conclave of Cardinals summoned for the purpose. It is interesting to note that the doubts thrown upon it seem to have been chiefly doubts about whether the rule was not too hard for humanity, for the Catholic Church is always on the watch against excessive asceticism and its evils. Probably they meant, especially when they said it was unduly hard, that it was unduly dangerous. For a certain element that can only be called danger is what marks the innovation as compared with older institutions of the kind. In one sense indeed the friar was almost the opposite of the monk. The value of the old monasticism had been that there was not only an ethical but an economic repose. Out of that repose had come the works for which the world will never be sufficiently grateful, the preservation of the classics, the beginning of the Gothic, the schemes of science and philosophies, the illuminated manuscripts and the coloured glass. The whole point of a monk was that his economic affairs were settled for good; he knew where he would get his supper, though it was a very plain supper. But the whole point of a friar was that he did not know where he would get his supper. There was always a possibility that he might get no supper. There was an element of what would be called romance, as of the gipsy or adventurer. But there was also an element of potential tragedy, as of the tramp or the casual labourer. So the Cardinals of the thirteenth century were filled with compassion, seeing a few men entering of their own free will that estate to which the poor of the twentieth century are daily driven by cold coercion and moved on by the police.

Cardinal San Paolo seems to have argued more or less in this manner: it may be a hard life, but

after all it is the life apparently described as
ideal in the Gospel; make what compromises you
think wise or humane about that ideal; but do not
commit yourselves to saying that men shall *not*
fulfil that ideal if they can. We shall see the
importance of this argument when we come to
the whole of that higher aspect of the life of
St. Francis which may be called the Imitation of
Christ. The upshot of the discussion was that the
Pope gave his verbal approval to the project and
promised a more definite endorsement, if the
movement should grow to more considerable
proportions. It is probable that Innocent, who
was himself a man of no ordinary mentality, had
very little doubt that it would do so; anyhow he
was not left long in doubt before it did do so.
The next passage in the history of the order is
simply the story of more and more people flock-
ing to its standard; and as has already been
remarked, once it had begun to grow, it could in
its nature grow much more quickly than any
ordinary society requiring ordinary funds and
public buildings. Even the return of the twelve
pioneers from their papal audience seems to have
been a sort of triumphal procession. In one place
in particular, it is said, the whole population of
a town, men, women and children, turned out,
leaving their work and wealth and homes exactly
as they stood and begging to be taken into the
army of God on the spot. According to the story,

it was on this occasion that St. Francis first fore-shadowed his idea of the Third Order which enabled men to share in the movement without leaving the homes and habits of normal humanity. For the moment it is most important to regard this story as one example of the riot of conversion with which he was already filling all the roads of Italy. It was a world of wandering; friars per-petually coming and going in all the highways and byways, seeking to ensure that any man who met one of them by chance should have a spiritual adventure. The First Order of St. Francis had entered history.

This rough outline can only be rounded off here with some description of the Second and Third Orders, though they were founded later and at separate times. The former was an order for women and owed its existence, of course, to the beautiful friendship of St. Francis and St. Clare. There is no story about which even the most sympathetic critics of another creed have been more bewildered and misleading. For there is no story that more clearly turns on that simple test which I have taken as crucial throughout this criticism. I mean that what is the matter with these critics is that they will not believe that a heavenly love can be as real as an earthly love. The moment it is treated as real, like an earthly love, their whole riddle is easily resolved. A girl of seventeen, named Clare and belonging to one of the noble families of Assisi, was filled with an enthusiasm for the conventual life; and Francis helped her to escape from her home and to take up the conventual life. If we like to put it so, he helped her to elope into the cloister, defying her parents as he had defied his father. Indeed the scene had many of the elements of a regular romantic elopement; for she escaped through a hole in the wall, fled through a wood and was received at midnight by the light of torches. Even Mrs. Oliphant, in her fine and delicate study of St. Francis, calls it " an incident which we can hardly record with satisfaction."

Now about that incident I will here only say this. If it had really been a romantic elopement and the girl had become a bride instead of a nun, practically the whole modern world would have made her a heroine. If the action of the Friar towards Clare had been the action of the Friar towards Juliet, everybody would be sympathising with her exactly as they sympathise with Juliet. It is not conclusive to say that Clare was only seventeen. Juliet was only fourteen. Girls married and boys fought in battles at such early ages in medieval times; and a girl of seventeen in the thirteenth century was certainly old enough to know her own mind. There cannot be the shadow of a doubt, for any sane person considering subsequent events, that St. Clare did know her own mind. But the point for the moment is that modern romanticism entirely encourages such defiance of parents when it is done in the name of romantic love. For it knows that romantic love is a reality, but it does not know that divine love is a reality. There may have been something to be said for the parents of Clare; there may have been something to be said for Peter Bernardone. So there may have been a great deal to be said for the Montagues or the Capulets; but the modern world does not want it said; and does not say it. The fact is that as soon as we assume for a moment as a hypothesis, what St. Francis and St. Clare assumed all the time as an absolute, that there is a direct divine relation more glorious than any romance, the story of St. Clare's elopement is simply a romance with a happy ending; and St. Francis is the St. George or knight-errant who gave it a happy ending. And seeing that some millions of men and women have lived and died treating this relation as a reality, a man is not much of a philosopher if he cannot even treat it as a hypothesis.

For the rest, we may at least assume that no friend of what is called the emancipation of women will regret the revolt of St. Clare. She did most truly, in the modern jargon, live her own life, the life that she herself wanted to lead, as distinct from the life into which parental commands and conventional arrangements would have forced her. She became the foundress of a great feminine movement which still profoundly affects the world; and her place is with the powerful women of history. It is not clear that she would have been so great or so useful if she had made a runaway match, or even stopped at home and made a *mariage de convenance.* So much any sensible man may well say considering the matter merely from the outside; and I have no intention of attempting to consider it from the inside. If a man may well doubt whether he is worthy to write a word about St. Francis, he will certainly want words better than his own to speak of the friendship of St. Francis and St. Clare. I have often remarked that the mysteries of this story are best expressed symbolically in certain silent attitudes and actions. And I know no better symbol than that found by the felicity of popular legend, which says that one night the people of Assisi thought the trees and the holy house were on fire, and rushed up to extinguish the conflagration. But they found all quiet within, where St. Francis broke bread with St. Clare at one of their rare meetings, and talked of the love of God. It would be hard to find a more imaginative image, for some sort of utterly pure and disembodied passion, than that red halo round the unconscious figures on the hill; a flame feeding on nothing and setting the very air on fire.

But if the Second Order was the memorial of such an unearthly love, the Third Order was as

I

solid a memorial of a very solid sympathy with
earthly loves and earthly lives.   The whole of this
feature in Catholic life, the lay orders in touch
with clerical orders, is very little understood in
Protestant countries and very little allowed for in
Protestant history.   The vision which has been
so faintly suggested in these pages has never been
confined to monks or even to friars.   It has been
an inspiration to innumerable crowds of ordinary
married men and women; living lives like our
own, only entirely different.   That morning glory
which St. Francis spread over earth and sky has
lingered as a secret sunshine under a multitude of
roofs and in a multitude of rooms.   In societies
like ours nothing is known of such a Franciscan
following.   Nothing is known of such obscure
followers; and if possible less is known of the well-
known followers.   If we imagine passing us in the
street a pageant of the Third Order of St. Francis,
the famous figures would surprise us more than
the strange ones.   For us it would be like the
unmasking of some mighty secret society.   There
rides St. Louis, the great king, lord of the higher
justice whose scales hang crooked in favour of the
poor.   There is Dante crowned with laurel, the
poet who in his life of passions sang the praises of
the Lady Poverty, whose grey garment is lined
with purple and all glorious within.   All sorts of
great names from the most recent and rationalistic centuries would stand revealed; the great

Galvani, for instance, the father of all electricity, the magician who has made so many modern systems of stars and sounds. So various a following would alone be enough to prove that St. Francis had no lack of sympathy with normal men, if the whole of his own life did not prove it.

But in fact his life did prove it, and that possibly in a more subtle sense. There is, I fancy, some truth in the hint of one of his modern biographers, that even his natural passions were singularly normal and even noble, in the sense of turning towards things not unlawful in themselves but only unlawful for him. Nobody ever lived of whom we could less fitly use the word " regret " than Francis of Assisi. Though there was much that was romantic, there was nothing in the least sentimental about his mood. It was not melancholy enough for that. He was of far too swift and rushing a temper to be troubled with doubts and reconsiderations about the race he ran; though he had any amount of self-reproach about not running faster. But it is true, one suspects, that when he wrestled with the devil, as every man must to be worth calling a man, the whispers referred mostly to those healthy instincts that he would have approved for others; they bore no resemblance to that ghastly painted paganism which sent its demoniac courtesans to plague St. Anthony in the desert. If St. Francis had only pleased himself, it would have been with simpler pleasures. He was moved to love rather than lust, and by nothing wilder than wedding-bells. It is suggested in that strange story of how he defied the devil by making images in the snow, and crying out that these sufficed him for a wife and family. It is suggested in the saying he used when disclaiming any security from sin, " I may yet have children "; almost as if it was of the children rather than the woman that he dreamed. And this, if it be true, gives a final touch to the truth about his character. There was so much about him of the spirit of the morning, so much that was curiously young and clean, that even what was bad in him was good. As it was said of others that the light in their body was darkness, so it may be said of this luminous spirit that the very shadows in his soul were of light. Evil itself could not come to him save in the form of a forbidden good; and he could only be tempted by a sacrament.

No man who has been given the freedom of the Faith is likely to fall into those hole-and-corner extravagances in which later degenerate Franciscans, or rather Fraticelli, sought to concentrate entirely on St. Francis as a second Christ, the creator of a new gospel. In fact any such notion makes nonsense of every motive in the man's life; for no man would reverently magnify what he was meant to rival, or only profess to follow what he existed to supplant. On the contrary, as will appear later, this little study would rather specially insist that it was really the papal sagacity that saved the great Franciscan movement for the whole world and the universal Church, and prevented it from petering out as that sort of stale and second-rate sect that is called a new religion. Everything that is written here must be understood not only as distinct from but diametrically opposed to the idolatry of the Fraticelli. The difference between Christ and St. Francis was the difference between the Creator and the creature;

and certainly no creature was ever so conscious of that colossal contrast as St. Francis
himself. But subject to this understanding,
it is perfectly true and it is vitally important
that Christ was the pattern on which St. Francis
sought to fashion himself; and that at many
points their human and historical lives were even
curiously coincident; and above all, that compared to most of us at least St. Francis is a most
sublime approximation to his Master, and,
even in being an intermediary and a reflection,
is a splendid and yet a merciful Mirror of
Christ. And this truth suggests another, which
I think has hardly been noticed; but which
happens to be a highly forcible argument for
the authority of Christ being continuous in the
Catholic Church.

Cardinal Newman wrote in his liveliest controversial work a sentence that might be a model
of what we mean by saying that his creed tends
to lucidity and logical courage. In speaking of
the ease with which truth may be made to look
like its own shadow or sham, he said, " And if
Antichrist is like Christ, Christ I suppose is
like Antichrist." Mere religious sentiment might
well be shocked at the end of the sentence;
but nobody could object to it except the logician
who said that Cæsar and Pompey were very
much alike, especially Pompey. It may give a
much milder shock if I say here, what most of

us have forgotten, that if St. Francis was like Christ, Christ was to that extent like St. Francis. And my present point is that it is really very enlightening to realise that Christ was like St. Francis. What I mean is this; that if men find certain riddles and hard sayings in the story of Galilee, and if they find the answers to those riddles in the story of Assisi, it really does show that a secret has been handed down in one religious tradition and no other. It shows that the casket that was locked in Palestine can be unlocked in Umbria; for the Church is the keeper of the keys.

Now in truth while it has always seemed natural to explain St. Francis in the light of Christ, it has not occurred to many people to explain Christ in the light of St. Francis. Perhaps the word " light " is not here the proper metaphor; but the same truth is admitted in the accepted metaphor of the mirror. St. Francis is the mirror of Christ rather as the moon is the mirror of the sun. The moon is much smaller than the sun, but it is also much nearer to us; and being less vivid it is more visible. Exactly in the same sense St. Francis is nearer to us, and being a mere man like ourselves is in that sense more imaginable. Being necessarily less of a mystery, he does not, for us, so much open his mouth in mysteries. Yet as a matter of fact, many minor things that seem mysteries in the

mouth of Christ would seem merely characteristic paradoxes in the mouth of St. Francis.
It seems natural to re-read the more remote
incidents with the help of the more recent ones.
It is a truism to say that Christ lived before
Christianity; and it follows that as an historical
figure He is a figure in heathen history. I mean
that the medium in which He moved was not the
medium of Christendom but of the old pagan
empire; and from that alone, not to mention
the distance of time, it follows that His circumstances are more alien to us than those of an
Italian monk such as we might meet even to-day.
I suppose the most authoritative commentary
can hardly be certain of the current or conventional weight of all His words or phrases; of
which of them would then have seemed a common
allusion and which a strange fancy. This archaic
setting has left many of the sayings standing
like hieroglyphics and subject to many and
peculiar individual interpretations. Yet it is
true of almost any of them that if we simply
translate them into the Umbrian dialect of the
first Franciscans, they would seem like any
other part of the Franciscan story; doubtless
in one sense fantastic, but quite familiar. All
sorts of critical controversies have revolved
round the passage which bids men consider the
lilies of the field and copy them in taking no
thought for the morrow. The sceptic has alter-

nated between telling us to be true Christians
and do it, and explaining that it is impossible
to do. When he is a communist as well as an
atheist, he is generally doubtful whether to
blame us for preaching what is impracticable
or for not instantly putting it into practice. I
am not going to discuss here the point of ethics
and economics; I merely remark that even
those who are puzzled at the saying of Christ
would hardly pause in accepting it as a saying
of St. Francis. Nobody would be surprised to
find that he had said, "I beseech you, little
brothers, that you be as wise as Brother Daisy
and Brother Dandelion; for never do they lie
awake thinking of to-morrow, yet they have
gold crowns like kings and emperors or like
Charlemagne in all his glory." Even more
bitterness and bewilderment has arisen about
the command to turn the other cheek and to
give the coat to the robber who has taken the
cloak. It is widely held to imply the wickedness
of war among nations; about which, in itself,
not a word seems to have been said. Taken thus
literally and universally, it much more clearly
implies the wickedness of all law and government.
Yet there are many prosperous peacemakers who
are much more shocked at the idea of using the
brute force of soldiers against a powerful foreigner
than they are at using the brute force of police-
men against a poor fellow-citizen. Here again I

am content to point out that the paradox becomes
perfectly human and probable if addressed by
Francis to Franciscans. Nobody would be surprised to read that Brother Juniper did then
run after the thief that had stolen his hood,
beseeching him to take his gown also; for so
St. Francis had commanded him. Nobody would
be surprised if St. Francis told a young noble,
about to be admitted to his company, that so
far from pursuing a brigand to recover his shoes,
he ought to pursue him to make him a present
of his stockings. We may like or not the atmosphere these things imply; but we know what
atmosphere they do imply. We recognise a
certain note as natural and clear as the note of
a bird; the note of St. Francis. There is in it
something of gentle mockery of the very idea of
possessions; something of a hope of disarming
the enemy by generosity; something of a humorous sense of bewildering the worldly with the
unexpected; something of the joy of carrying
an enthusiastic conviction to a logical extreme.
But anyhow we have no difficulty in recognising
it, if we have read any of the literature of the
Little Brothers and the movement that began
in Assisi. It seems reasonable to infer that if
it was this spirit that made such strange things
possible in Umbria, it was the same spirit that
made them possible in Palestine. If we hear
the same unmistakable note and sense the same

indescribable savour in two things at such a distance from each other, it seems natural to suppose that the case that is more remote from our experience was like the case that is closer to our experience. As the thing is explicable on the assumption that Francis was speaking to Franciscans, it is not an irrational explanation to suggest that Christ also was speaking to some dedicated band that had much the same function as Franciscans. In other words, it seems only natural to hold, as the Catholic Church has held, that these counsels of perfection were part of a particular vocation to astonish and awaken the world. But in any case it is important to note that when we do find these particular features, with their seemingly fantastic fitness, reappearing after more than a thousand years, we find them produced by the same religious system which claims continuity and authority from the scenes in which they first appeared. Any number of philosophies will repeat the platitudes of Christianity. But it is the ancient Church that can again startle the world with the paradoxes of Christianity. *Ubi Petrus ibi Franciscus.*

But if we understand that it was truly under the inspiration of his divine Master that St. Francis did these merely quaint or eccentric acts of charity, we must understand that it was under the same inspiration that he did acts of self-denial and austerity. It is clear that these more or less playful parables of the love of men were conceived after a close study of the Sermon on the Mount. But it is evident that he made an even closer study of the silent sermon on that other mountain; the mountain that was called Golgotha. Here again he was speaking the strict historical truth, when he said that in fasting or suffering humiliation he was but trying to do something of what Christ did; and here again it seems probable that as the same truth appears at the two ends of a chain of tradition, the tradition has preserved the truth. But the import of this fact at the moment affects the next phase in the personal history of the man himself.

For as it becomes clearer that his great communal scheme is an accomplished fact and past the peril of an early collapse, as it becomes evident that there already is such a thing as an Order of the Friars Minor, this more individual and intense ambition of St. Francis emerges more and more. So soon as he certainly has followers, he does not compare himself with his followers, towards whom he might appear as a master; he compares himself more and more with his Master, towards whom he appears only as a servant. This, it may be said in passing, is one of the moral and even practical conveniences of the ascetical privilege. Every other sort of superiority may be superciliousness.

But the saint is never supercilious, for he is always by hypothesis in the presence of a superior. The objection to an aristocracy is that it is a priesthood without a god. But in any case the service to which St. Francis had committed himself was one which, about this time, he conceived more and more in terms of sacrifice and crucifixion. He was full of the sentiment that he had not suffered enough to be worthy even to be a distant follower of his suffering God. And this passage in his history may really be roughly summarised as the Search for Martyrdom.

This was the ultimate idea in the remarkable business of his expedition among the Saracens in Syria. There were indeed other elements in his conception, which are worthy of more intelligent understanding than they have often received. His idea, of course, was to bring the Crusades in a double sense to their end; that is, to reach their conclusion and to achieve their purpose. Only he wished to do it by conversion and not by conquest; that is, by intellectual and not material means. The modern mind is hard to please; and it generally calls the way of Godfrey ferocious and the way of Francis fanatical. That is, it calls any moral method unpractical, when it has just called any practical method immoral. But the idea of St. Francis was far from being a fanatical or necessarily even an unpractical idea; though perhaps he saw the problem as rather too simple, lacking the learning of his great inheritor Raymond Lully, who understood more but has been quite as little understood. The way he approached the matter was indeed highly personal and peculiar; but that was true of almost everything he did. It was in one way a simple idea, as most of his ideas were simple ideas. But it was not a silly idea; there was a great deal to be said for it and it might have succeeded. It was, of course, simply the idea that it is better to create Christians than to destroy Moslems. If Islam had been converted, the world would have been immeasurably more united and happy; for one thing, three quarters of the wars of modern history would never have taken place. It was not absurd to suppose that this might be effected, without military force, by missionaries who were also martyrs. The Church had conquered Europe in that way and may yet conquer Asia or Africa in that way. But when all this is allowed for, there is still another sense in which St. Francis was not thinking of Martyrdom as a means to an end, but almost as an end in itself; in the sense that to him the supreme end was to come closer to the example of Christ. Through all his plunging and restless days ran the refrain: I have not suffered enough; I have not sacrificed enough; I am not yet worthy even of the shadow of the crown of thorns. He wandered about the valleys of the world looking for the hill that has the outline of a skull.

A little while before his final departure for the East a vast and triumphant assembly of the whole order had been held near the Portiuncula; and called The Assembly of the Straw Huts, from the manner in which that mighty army encamped in the field. Tradition says that it was on this occasion that St. Francis met St. Dominic for the first and last time. It also says, what is probable enough, that the practical spirit of the Spaniard was almost appalled at the devout irresponsibility of the Italian, who had assembled such a crowd without organising a commissariat. Dominic the Spaniard was, like nearly every Spaniard, a man with the mind of a soldier. His charity took the practical form of provision and preparation. But, apart from the disputes about faith which such incidents open, he probably did not understand in this case the power of mere popularity produced by mere personality. In all his leaps in the dark, Francis had an extraordinary faculty of falling on his feet. The whole countryside came down like a landslide to provide food and drink for this sort of pious picnic. Peasants brought waggons of wine and game; great nobles walked about doing the work of footmen. It was a very real victory for the Franciscan spirit of a reckless faith not only in God but in

man. Of course there is much doubt and dispute
about the whole story and the whole relation
of Francis and Dominic; and the story of the
Assembly of the Straw Huts is told from the
Franciscan side. But the alleged meeting is
worth mentioning, precisely because it was
immediately before St. Francis set forth on his
bloodless crusade that he is said to have met
St. Dominic, who has been so much criticised for
lending himself to a more bloody one. There
is no space in this little book to explain how
St. Francis, as much as St. Dominic, would
ultimately have defended the defence of Christian
unity by arms. Indeed it would need a large
book instead of a little book to develop that
point alone from its first principles. For the
modern mind is merely a blank about the philosophy of toleration; and the average agnostic
of recent times has really had no notion of what
he meant by religious liberty and equality.
He took his own ethics as self-evident and enforced
them; such as decency or the error of the Adamite
heresy. Then he was horribly shocked if he heard
of anybody else, Moslem or Christian, taking
his ethics as self-evident and enforcing *them;*
such as reverence or the error of the Atheist
heresy. And then he wound up by taking all
this lop-sided illogical deadlock, of the unconscious meeting the unfamiliar, and called it
the liberality of his own mind. Medieval men

thought that if a social system was founded on a certain idea it must fight for that idea, whether it was as simple as Islam or as carefully balanced as Catholicism. Modern men really think the same thing, as is clear when communists attack their ideas of property. Only they do not think it so clearly, because they have not really thought out their idea of property. But while it is probable that St. Francis would have reluctantly agreed with St. Dominic that war for the truth was right in the last resort, it is certain that St. Dominic did enthusiastically agree with St. Francis that it was far better to prevail by persuasion and enlightenment if it were possible. St. Dominic devoted himself much more to persuading than to persecuting; but there was a difference in the methods simply because there was a difference in the men. About everything St. Francis did there was something that was in a good sense childish, and even in a good sense wilful. He threw himself into things abruptly, as if they had just occurred to him. He made a dash for his Mediterranean enterprise with something of the air of a schoolboy running away to sea.

In the first act of that attempt he characteristically distinguished himself by becoming the Patron Saint of Stowaways. He never thought of waiting for introductions or bargains or any of the considerable backing that he already had

K

from rich and responsible people. He simply saw a boat and threw himself into it, as he threw himself into everything else. It has all that air of running a race which makes his whole life read like an escapade or even literally an escape. He lay like lumber among the cargo, with one companion whom he had swept with him in his rush; but the voyage was apparently unfortunate and erratic and ended in an enforced return to Italy. Apparently it was after this first false start that the great re-union took place at the Portiuncula, and between this and the final Syrian journey there was also an attempt to meet the Moslem menace by preaching to the Moors in Spain. In Spain indeed several of the first Franciscans had already succeeded gloriously in being martyred. But the great Francis still went about stretching out his arms for such torments and desiring that agony in vain. No one would have said more readily than he that he was probably less like Christ than those others who had already found their Calvary; but the thing remained with him like a secret; the strangest of the sorrows of man.

His later voyage was more successful, so far as arriving at the scene of operations was concerned. He arrived at the headquarters of the Crusade which was in front of the besieged city of Damietta, and went on in his rapid and

solitary fashion to seek the headquarters of the
Saracens. He succeeded in obtaining an interview with the Sultan; and it was at that interview
that he evidently offered, and as some say proceeded, to fling himself into the fire as a divine
ordeal, defying the Moslem religious teachers
to do the same. It is quite certain that he would
have done so at a moment's notice. Indeed
throwing himself into the fire was hardly more
desperate, in any case, than throwing himself
among the weapons and tools of torture of a
horde of fanatical Mahomedans and asking them
to renounce Mahomet. It is said further that
the Mahomedan muftis showed some coldness
towards the proposed competition, and that one
of them quietly withdrew while it was under
discussion; which would also appear credible.
But for whatever reason Francis evidently
returned as freely as he came. There may be
something in the story of the individual impression produced on the Sultan, which the narrator
represents as a sort of secret conversion. There
may be something in the suggestion that the
holy man was unconsciously protected among
half-barbarous orientals by the halo of sanctity
that is supposed in such places to surround an
idiot. There is probably as much or more in
the more generous explanation of that graceful
though capricious courtesy and compassion which
mingled with wilder things in the stately Soldans

of the type and tradition of Saladin. Finally,
there is perhaps something in the suggestion
that the tale of St. Francis might be told as a
sort of ironic tragedy and comedy called The
Man Who Could Not Get Killed.   Men liked
him too much for himself to let him die for his
faith; and the man was received instead of the
message. But all these are only converging
guesses at a great effort that is hard to judge,
because it broke off short like the beginnings of
a great bridge that might have united East and
West, and remains one of the great might-have-
beens of history.

Meanwhile the great movement in Italy was
making giant strides. Backed now by papal
authority as well as popular enthusiasm, and
creating a kind of comradeship among all classes,
it had started a riot of reconstruction on all
sides of religious and social life; and especially
began to express itself in that enthusiasm for
building which is the mark of all the resur-
rections of Western Europe. There had notably
been established at Bologna a magnificent mission
house of the Friars Minor; and a vast body of
them and their sympathisers surrounded it with
a chorus of acclamation. Their unanimity had
a strange interruption. One man alone in that
crowd was seen to turn and suddenly denounce
the building as if it had been a Babylonian temple;
demanding indignantly since when the Lady

Poverty had thus been insulted with the luxury of palaces. It was Francis, a wild figure, returned from his Eastern Crusade; and it was the first and last time that he spoke in wrath to his children.

A word must be said later about this serious division of sentiment and policy, about which many Franciscans, and to some extent Francis himself, parted company with the more moderate policy which ultimately prevailed. At this point we need only note it as another shadow fallen upon his spirit after his disappointment in the desert; and as in some sense the prelude to the next phase of his career, which is the most isolated and the most mysterious. It is true that everything about this episode seems to be covered with some cloud of dispute, even including its date; some writers putting it much earlier in the narrative than this. But whether or no it was chronologically it was certainly logically the culmination of the story, and may best be indicated here. I say indicated for it must be a matter of little more than indication; the thing being a mystery both in the higher moral and the more trivial historical sense. Anyhow the conditions of the affair seem to have been these. Francis and a young companion, in the course of their common wandering, came past a great castle all lighted up with the festivities attending a son of the house receiving the honour of knighthood. This aristocratic mansion, which took its name from Monte Feltro, they entered in their beautiful and casual fashion and began to give their own sort of good news. There were some at least who listened to the saint " as if he had been an angel of God "; among them a gentleman named Orlando of Chiusi, who had great lands in Tuscany, and who proceeded to do St. Francis a singular and somewhat picturesque act of courtesy. He gave him a mountain; a thing somewhat unique among the gifts of the world. Presumably the Franciscan rule which forbade a man to accept money had made no detailed provision about accepting mountains. Nor indeed did St. Francis accept it save as he accepted everything, as a temporary convenience rather than a personal possession; but he turned it into a sort of refuge for the eremitical rather than the monastic life; he retired there when he wished for a life of prayer and fasting which he did not ask even his closest friends to follow. This was Alverno of the Apennines, and upon its peak there rests for ever a dark cloud that has a rim or halo of glory.

What it was exactly that happened there may never be known. The matter has been, I believe, a subject of dispute among the most devout students of the saintly life as well as between such students and others of the more secular sort. It may be that St. Francis never spoke to a soul on the subject; it would be highly characteristic,

and it is certain in any case that he said very
little; I think he is only alleged to have spoken
of it to one man. Subject however to such truly
sacred doubts, I will confess that to me personally
this one solitary and indirect report that has
come down to us reads very like the report of
something real; of some of those things that
are more real than what we call daily realities.
Even something as it were double and bewildering
about the image seems to carry the impression
of an experience shaking the senses; as does the
passage in Revelations about the supernatural
creatures full of eyes. It would seem that St.
Francis beheld the heavens above him occupied
by a vast winged being like a seraph spread out
like a cross. There seems some mystery about
whether the winged figure was itself crucified
or in the posture of crucifixion, or whether it
merely enclosed in its frame of wings some
colossal crucifix. But it seems clear that there
was some question of the former impression;
for St. Bonaventura distinctly says that St.
Francis doubted how a seraph could be crucified,
since those awful and ancient principalities
were without the infirmity of the Passion. St.
Bonaventura suggests that the seeming contradiction may have meant that St. Francis
was to be crucified as a spirit since he could not
be crucified as a man; but whatever the meaning
of the vision, the general idea of it is very vivid

and overwhelming. St. Francis saw above him, filling the whole heavens, some vast immemorial unthinkable power, ancient like the Ancient of Days, whose calm men had conceived under the forms of winged bulls or monstrous cherubim, and all that winged wonder was in pain like a wounded bird. This seraphic suffering, it is said, pierced his soul with a sword of grief and pity; it may be inferred that some sort of mounting agony accompanied the ecstasy. Finally after some fashion the apocalypse faded from the sky and the agony within subsided; and silence and the natural air filled the morning twilight and settled slowly in the purple chasms and cleft abysses of the Apennines.

The head of the solitary sank, amid all that relaxation and quiet in which time can drift by with the sense of something ended and complete; and as he stared downwards, he saw the marks of nails in his own hands.

THE tremendous story of the Stigmata of St. Francis, which was the end of the last chapter, was in some sense the end of his life. In a logical sense, it would have been the end even if it had happened at the beginning. But truer traditions refer it to a later date and suggest that his remaining days on the earth had something about them of the lingering of a shadow. Whether St. Bonaventura was right in his hint that St. Francis saw in that seraphic vision something almost like a vast mirror of his own soul, that could at least suffer like an angel though not like a god, or whether it expressed under an imagery more primitive and colossal than common Christian art the primary paradox of the death of God, it is evident from its traditional consequences that it was meant for a crown and for a seal. It seems to have been after seeing this vision that he began to go blind.

But the incident has another and much less important place in this rough and limited outline. It is the natural occasion for considering

briefly and collectively all the facts or fables of
another aspect of the life of St. Francis; an aspect
which is, I will not say more disputable, but
certainly more disputed. I mean all that mass
of testimony and tradition that concerns his
miraculous powers and supernatural experiences,
with which it would have been easy to stud and
bejewel every page of the story; only that
certain circumstances necessary to the conditions
of this narration make it better to gather, somewhat hastily, all such jewels into a heap.

I have here adopted this course in order to
make allowance for a prejudice. It is indeed to
a great extent a prejudice of the past; a prejudice
that is plainly disappearing in days of greater
enlightenment, and especially of a greater range
of scientific experiment and knowledge. But it
is a prejudice that is still tenacious in many of
an older generation and still traditional in many
of the younger. I mean, of course, what used
to be called the belief " that miracles do not
happen," as I think Matthew Arnold expressed
it, in expressing the standpoint of so many of
our Victorian uncles and great-uncles. In other
words it was the remains of that sceptical simplification by which some of the philosophers of the
early eighteenth century had popularised the
impression (for a very short time) that we had
discovered the regulations of the cosmos like the
works of a clock, of so very simple a clock that

it was possible to distinguish almost at a glance what could or could not have happened in human experience. It should be remembered that these real sceptics, of the golden age of scepticism, were quite as scornful of the first fancies of science as of the lingering legends of religion. Voltaire, when he was told that a fossil fish had been found on the peaks of the Alps, laughed openly at the tale and said that some fasting monk or hermit had dropped his fish-bones there; possibly in order to effect another monkish fraud. Everybody knows by this time that science has had its revenge on scepticism. The border between the credible and the incredible has not only become once more as vague as in any barbaric twilight; but the credible is obviously increasing and the incredible shrinking. A man in Voltaire's time did not know what miracle he would next have to throw up. A man in our time does not know what miracle he will next have to swallow.

But long before these things had happened, in those days of my boyhood when I first saw the figure of St. Francis far away in the distance and drawing me even at that distance, in those Victorian days which did seriously separate the virtues from the miracles of the saints—even in those days I could not help feeling vaguely puzzled about how this method could be applied to history. Even then I did not quite understand, and even now I do not quite understand, on what principle one is to pick and choose in the chronicles of the past which seem to be all of a piece. All our knowledge of certain historical periods, and notably of the whole medieval period, rests on certain connected chronicles written by people who are some of them nameless and all of them dead, who cannot in any case be cross-examined and cannot in some cases be corroborated. I have never been quite clear about the nature of the right by which historians accepted masses of detail from them as definitely true, and suddenly denied their truthfulness when one detail was preternatural. I do not complain of their being sceptics; I am puzzled about why the sceptics are not more sceptical. I can understand their saying that these details would never have been included in a chronicle except by lunatics or liars; but in that case the only inference is that the chronicle was written by liars or lunatics. They will write for instance: " Monkish fanaticism found it easy to spread the report that miracles were already being worked at the tomb of Thomas Becket." Why should they not say equally well, " Monkish fanaticism found it easy to spread the slander that four knights from King Henry's court had assassinated Thomas Becket in the cathedral " ? They would write something like this : " The credulity of the age readily believed that Joan of Arc had been inspired to point out the Dauphin although he was in disguise." Why should they not write on the same principle : " The credulity of the age was such as to suppose that an obscure peasant girl could get an audience at the court of the Dauphin "? And so, in the present case, when they tell us there is a wild story that St. Francis flung himself into the fire and emerged scathless, upon what precise principle are they forbidden to tell us of a wild story that St. Francis flung himself into the camp of the ferocious Moslems and returned safe? I only ask for information ; for I do not see the rationale of the thing myself. I will undertake to say there was not a word written of St. Francis by any contemporary who was himself incapable of believing and telling a miraculous story. Perhaps it is all monkish fables and there never was any St. Francis or any St. Thomas Becket or any Joan of Arc. This is undoubtedly a *reductio ad absurdum*; but it is a *reductio ad absurdum* of the view which thought all miracles absurd.

And in abstract logic this method of selection would lead to the wildest absurdities. An intrinsically incredible story could only mean that the authority was unworthy of credit. It could not mean that other parts of his story must be received with complete credulity. If somebody said he had met a man in yellow trousers, who proceeded to jump down his own throat, we should not exactly take our Bible oath or be burned at the stake for the statement that he wore yellow trousers. If somebody claimed to have gone up in a blue balloon and found that the moon was made of green cheese, we should not exactly take an affidavit that the balloon was blue any more than that the moon was green. And the really logical conclusion from throwing doubts on all tales like the miracles of St. Francis was to throw doubts on the existence of men like St. Francis. And there really was a modern moment, a sort of high-water mark of insane scepticism, when this sort of thing was really said or done. People used to go about saying that there was no such person as St. Patrick; which is every bit as much of a human and historical howler as saying there was no such person as St. Francis. There was a time, for instance, when the madness of mythological explanation had dissolved a large part of solid history under the universal and luxuriant warmth and radiance of the Sun-Myth. I believe that that particular sun has already set, but there have been any number of moons and meteors to take its place.

St. Francis, of course, would make a magnificent Sun-Myth. How could anybody miss the chance of being a Sun-Myth when he is actually best known by a song called The Canticle of the Sun? It is needless to point out that the fire in Syria was the dawn in the East and the bleeding wounds in Tuscany the sunset in the West. I could expound this theory at considerable length; only, as so often happens to such fine theorists, another and more promising theory occurs to me. I cannot think how everybody, including myself, can have overlooked the fact that the whole tale of St. Francis is of Totemistic origin. It is unquestionably a tale that simply swarms with totems. The Franciscan woods are as full of them as any Red Indian fable. Francis is made to call himself an ass, because in the original mythos Francis was merely the name given to the real four-footed donkey, afterwards vaguely evolved into a half-human god or hero. And that, no doubt, is why I used to feel that the Brother Wolf and Sister Bird of St. Francis were somehow like the Brer Fox and Sis Cow of Uncle Remus. Some say there is an innocent stage of infancy in which we do really believe that a cow talked or a fox made a tar baby. Anyhow there is an innocent period of intellectual growth in which we do sometimes really believe that St. Patrick was a Sun-Myth or St. Francis a Totem. But for the most of us both those phases of paradise are past.

As I shall suggest in a moment, there is one sense in which we can for practical purposes distinguish between probable and improbable things in such a story. It is not so much a

question of cosmic criticism about the nature of
the event as of literary criticism about the nature
of the story. Some stories are told much more
seriously than others. But apart from this, I
shall not attempt here any definite differentiation
between them. I shall not do so for a practical
reason affecting the utility of the proceeding; I
mean the fact that in a practical sense the whole
of this matter is again in the melting pot, from
which many things may emerge moulded into
what rationalism would have called monsters.
The fixed points of faith and philosophy do
indeed remain always the same. Whether a man
believes that fire in one case could fail to burn,
depends on why he thinks it generally does burn.
If it burns nine sticks out of ten because it is
its nature or doom to do so, then it will burn
the tenth stick as well. If it burns nine sticks
because it is the will of God that it should, then
it might be the will of God that the tenth should
be unburned. Nobody can get behind that
fundamental difference about the reason of
things; and it is as rational for a theist to
believe in miracles as for an atheist to disbelieve
in them. In other words there is only one
intelligent reason why a man does not believe in
miracles and that is that he does believe in
materialism. But these fixed points of faith and
philosophy are things for a theoretical work and
have no particular place here. And in the matter

of history and biography, which have their place here, nothing is fixed at all. The world is in a welter of the possible and impossible, and nobody knows what will be the next scientific hypothesis to support some ancient superstition. Three-quarters of the miracles attributed to St. Francis would already be explained by psychologists, not indeed as a Catholic explains them, but as a materialist must necessarily refuse to explain them. There is one whole department of the miracles of St. Francis; the miracles of healing. What is the good of a superior sceptic throwing them away as unthinkable, at the moment when faith-healing is already a big booming Yankee business like Barnum's Show? There is another whole department analogous to the tales of Christ " perceiving men's thoughts." What is the use of censoring them and blacking them out because they are marked " miracles," when thought-reading is already a parlour game like musical chairs? There is another whole department, to be studied separately if such scientific study were possible, of the well-attested wonders worked from his relics and fragmentary possessions. What is the use of dismissing all that as inconceivable, when even these common psychical parlour tricks turn perpetually upon touching some familiar object or holding in the hand some personal possession? I do not believe, of course, that these tricks are of the same type

L

as the good works of the saint; save perhaps in the sense of *Diabolus simius Dei*. But it is not a question of what I believe and why, but of what the sceptic disbelieves and why. And the moral for the practical biographer and historian is that he must wait till things settle down a little more, before he claims to disbelieve anything.

This being so he can choose between two courses; and not without some hesitation, I have here chosen between them. The best and boldest course would be to tell the whole story in a straightforward way, miracles and all, as the original historians told it. And to this sane and simple course the new historians will probably have to return. But it must be remembered that this book is avowedly only an introduction to St. Francis or the study of St. Francis. Those who need an introduction are in their nature strangers. With them the object is to get them to listen to St. Francis at all; and in doing so it is perfectly legitimate so to arrange the order of the facts that the familiar come before the unfamiliar and those they can at once understand before those they have a difficulty in understanding. I should only be too thankful if this thin and scratchy sketch contains a line or two that attracts men to study St. Francis for themselves; and if they do study him for themselves, they will soon find that the supernatural part of the story seems quite as natural as the rest. But it was necessary that my outline should be a merely human one, since I was only presenting his claim on all humanity, including sceptical humanity. I therefore adopted the alternative course, of showing first that nobody but a born fool could fail to realise that Francis of Assisi was a very real historical human being; and then summarising briefly in this chapter the superhuman powers that were certainly a part of that history and humanity. It only remains to say a few words about some distinctions that may reasonably be observed in the matter by any man of any views; that he may not confuse the point and climax of the saint's life with the fancies or rumours that were really only the fringes of his reputation.

There is so immense a mass of legends and anecdotes about St. Francis of Assisi, and there are so many admirable compilations that cover nearly all of them, that I have been compelled within these narrow limits to pursue a somewhat narrow policy; that of following one line of explanation and only mentioning one anecdote here or there because it illustrates that explanation. If this is true about all the legends and stories, it is especially true about the miraculous legends and the supernatural stories. If we were to take some stories as they stand, we should receive a rather bewildered impression that the biography contains more supernatural events than natural ones. Now it is clean against Catholic tradition, co-incident in so many points with common sense, to suppose that this is really the proportion of these things in practical human life. Moreover, even considered as supernatural or preternatural stories, they obviously fall into certain different classes, not so much by our experience of miracles as by our experience of stories. Some of them have the character of fairy stories, in their form even more than their incident. They are obviously tales told by the fire to peasants or the children of peasants, under conditions in which nobody thinks he is propounding a religious doctrine to be received or rejected, but only rounding off a story in the most symmetrical way, according to that sort of decorative scheme or pattern that runs through all fairy stories. Others are obviously in their form most emphatically evidence; that is they are testimony that is truth or lies; and it will be very hard for any judge of human nature to think they are lies.

It is admitted that the story of the Stigmata is not a legend but can only be a lie. I mean that it is certainly not a late legendary accretion added afterwards to the fame of St. Francis; but is something that started almost immediately with his earliest biographers. It is practically necessary to suggest that it was a conspiracy; indeed there has been some disposition to put

the fraud upon the unfortunate Elias, whom so
many parties have been disposed to treat as a
useful universal villain. It has been said, indeed,
that these early biographers, St. Bonaventura
and Celano and the Three Companions, though
they declare that St. Francis received the mystical
wounds, do not say that they themselves saw
those wounds. I do not think this argument
conclusive; because it only arises out of the very
nature of the narrative. The Three Companions
are not in any case making an affidavit; and
therefore none of the admitted parts of their
story are in the form of an affidavit. They are
writing a chronicle of a comparatively impersonal
and very objective description. They do not say,
" I saw St. Francis's wounds "; they say, " St.
Francis received wounds." But neither do they
say, " I saw St. Francis go into the Portiuncula ";
they say, " St. Francis went into the Portiuncula."
But I still cannot understand why they should be
trusted as eye-witnesses about the one fact and
not trusted as eye-witnesses about the other. It
is all of a piece; it would be a most abrupt and
abnormal interruption in their way of telling the
story if they suddenly began to curse and to
swear, and give their names and addresses, and
take their oath that they themselves saw and
verified the physical facts in question. It seems
to me, therefore, that this particular discussion
goes back to the general question I have already

mentioned; the question of why these chronicles should be credited at all, if they are credited with abounding in the incredible. But that again will probably be found to revert, in the last resort, to the mere fact that some men cannot believe in miracles because they are materialists. That is logical enough; but they are bound to deny the preternatural as much in the testimony of a modern scientific professor as in that of a medieval monkish chronicler. And there are plenty of professors for them to contradict by this time.

But whatever may be thought of such supernaturalism in the comparatively material and popular sense of supernatural acts, we shall miss the whole point of St. Francis, especially of St. Francis after Alverno, if we do not realise that he was living a supernatural life. And there is more and more of such supernaturalism in his life as he approaches towards his death. This element of the supernatural did not separate him from the natural; for it was the whole point of his position that it united him more perfectly to the natural. It did not make him dismal or dehumanised; for it was the whole meaning of his message that such mysticism makes a man cheerful and humane. But it was the whole point of his position, and it was the whole meaning of his message, that the power that did it was a supernatural power. If this simple dis-

tinction were not apparent from the whole of
his life, it would be difficult for anyone to miss
it in reading the account of his death.

In a sense he may be said to have wandered
as a dying man, just as he had wandered as a
living one. As it became more and more apparent
that his health was failing, he seems to have
been carried from place to place like a pageant
of sickness or almost like a pageant of mortality.
He went to Rieti, to Nursia, perhaps to Naples,
certainly to Cortona by the lake of Perugia.
But there is something profoundly pathetic, and
full of great problems, in the fact that at last,
as it would seem, his flame of life leapt up and
his heart rejoiced when they saw afar off on the
Assisian hill the solemn pillars of the Portiuncula.
He who had become a vagabond for the sake of
a vision, he who had denied himself all sense of
place and possession, he whose whole gospel and
glory it was to be homeless, received like a
Parthian shot from nature, the sting of the sense
of home. He also had his *maladie du clocher*,
his sickness of the spire; though his spire was
higher than ours. "Never," he cried with the
sudden energy of strong spirits in death, "never
give up this place. If you would go anywhere
or make any pilgrimage, return always to your
home; for this is the holy house of God." And
the procession passed under the arches of his
home; and he laid down on his bed and his

brethren gathered round him for the last long
vigil. It seems to me no moment for entering
into the subsequent disputes about which suc-
cessors he blessed or in what form and with
what significance. In that one mighty moment
he blessed us all.

After he had taken farewell of some of his
nearest and especially some of his oldest friends,
he was lifted at his own request off his own rude
bed and laid on the bare ground; as some say
clad only in a hair-shirt, as he had first gone
forth into the wintry woods from the presence of
his father. It was the final assertion of his great
fixed idea; of praise and thanks springing to
their most towering height out of nakedness and
nothing. As he lay there we may be certain
that his seared and blinded eyes saw nothing
but their object and their origin. We may be
sure that the soul, in its last inconceivable isolation, was face to face with nothing less than
God Incarnate and Christ Crucified. But for the
men standing around him there must have been
other thoughts mingling with these; and many
memories must have gathered like ghosts in the
twilight, as that day wore on and that great
darkness descended in which we all lost a friend.

For what lay dying there was not Dominic of
the Dogs of God, a leader in logical and controversial wars that could be reduced to a plan
and handed on like a plan; a master of a machine

of democratic discipline by which others could organise themselves. What was passing from the world was a person; a poet; an outlook on life like a light that was never after on sea or land; a thing not to be replaced or repeated while the earth endures. It has been said that there was only one Christian, who died on the cross; it is truer to say in this sense that there was only one Franciscan, whose name was Francis. Huge and happy as was the popular work he left behind him, there was something that he could not leave behind, any more than a landscape painter can leave his eyes in his will. It was an artist in life who was here called to be an artist in death; and he had a better right than Nero, his anti-type, to say *Qualis artifex pereo*. For Nero's life was full of posing for the occasion like that of an actor; while the Umbrian's had a natural and continuous grace like that of an athlete. But St. Francis had better things to say and better things to think about, and his thoughts were caught upwards where we cannot follow them, in divine and dizzy heights to which death alone can lift us up.

Round about him stood the brethren in their brown habits, those that had loved him even if they afterwards disputed with each other. There was Bernard his first friend and Angelo who had served as his secretary and Elias his successor, whom tradition tried to turn into a sort of Judas, but who seems to have been little worse than an official in the wrong place. His tragedy was that he had a Franciscan habit without a Franciscan heart, or at any rate with a very un-Franciscan head. But though he made a bad Franciscan, he might have made a decent Dominican. Anyhow, there is no reason to doubt that he loved Francis, for ruffians and savages did that. Anyhow he stood among the rest as the hours passed and the shadows lengthened in the house of the Portiuncula; and nobody need think so ill of him as to suppose that his thoughts were then in the tumultuous future, in the ambitions and controversies of his later years.

A man might fancy that the birds must have known when it happened; and made some motion in the evening sky. As they had once, according to the tale, scattered to the four winds of heaven in the pattern of a cross at his signal of dispersion, they might now have written in such dotted lines a more awful augury across the sky. Hidden in the woods perhaps were little cowering creatures never again to be so much noticed and understood; and it has been said that animals are sometimes conscious of things to which man their spiritual superior is for the moment blind. We do not know whether any shiver passed through all the thieves and the outcasts and the outlaws, to tell them what had happened to him who never knew the nature of scorn. But at least in the passages and porches of the Portiuncula there was a sudden stillness, where all the brown figures stood like bronze statues; for the stopping of the great heart that had not broken till it held the world.

IN one sense doubtless it is a sad irony that St. Francis, who all his life had desired all men to agree, should have died amid increasing disagreements. But we must not exaggerate this discord, as some have done, so as to turn it into a mere defeat of all his ideals. There are some who represent his work as having been merely ruined by the wickedness of the world, or what they always assume to be the even greater wickedness of the Church.

This little book is an essay on St. Francis and not on the Franciscan Order, still less on the Catholic Church or the Papacy or the policy pursued towards the extreme Franciscans or the Fraticelli. It is therefore only necessary to note in a very few words what was the general nature of the controversy that raged after the great saint's death, and to some extent troubled the last days of his life. The dominant detail was the interpretation of the vow of poverty, or the refusal of all possessions. Nobody so far as I know ever proposed to interfere with the vow of the individual friar that he would have no individual possessions. Nobody, that is, proposed to interfere with his negation of private property. But some Franciscans, invoking the authority of Francis on their side, went further than this and further I think than anybody else has ever gone. They proposed to abolish not only private property but property. That is, they refused to be corporately responsible for anything at all; for any buildings or stores or tools; they refused to own them collectively even when they used them collectively. It is perfectly true that many, especially among the first supporters of this view, were men of a splendid and selfless spirit, wholly devoted to the great saint's ideal. It is also perfectly true that the Pope and the authorities of the Church did not think this conception was a workable arrangement, and went so far in modifying it as to set aside certain clauses in the great saint's will. But it is not at all easy to see that it *was* a workable arrangement or even an arrangement at all; for it was really a refusal to arrange anything. Everybody knew of course that Franciscans were communists; but this was not so much being a communist as being an anarchist. Surely upon any argument somebody or something must be answerable for what happened to or in or concerning a number of historic edifices and ordinary goods and chattels. Many idealists of a social-

istic sort, notably of the school of Mr. Shaw or
Mr. Wells, have treated this dispute as if it were
merely a case of the tyranny of wealthy and wicked
pontiffs crushing the true Christianity of Christian
Socialists. But in truth this extreme ideal was
in a sense the very reverse of Socialist, or even
social. Precisely the thing which these enthusiasts
refused was that social ownership on which
Socialism is built; what they primarily refused
to do was what Socialists primarily exist to do;
to own legally in their corporate capacity. Nor
is it true that the tone of the Popes towards the
enthusiasts was merely harsh and hostile. The
Pope maintained for a long time a compromise
which he had specially designed to meet their
own conscientious objections; a compromise
by which the Papacy itself held the property
in a kind of trust for the owners who refused
to touch it. The truth is that this incident
shows two things which are common enough
in Catholic history, but very little understood
by the journalistic history of industrial civilisation. It shows that the Saints were sometimes
great men when the Popes were small men. But
it also shows that great men are sometimes
wrong when small men are right. And it will be
found, after all, very difficult for any candid
and clear-headed outsider to deny that the Pope
was right, when he insisted that the world was
not made only for Franciscans.

For that was what was behind the quarrel. At the back of this particular practical question there was something much larger and more momentous, the stir and wind of which we can feel as we read the controversy. We might go so far as to put the ultimate truth thus. St. Francis was so great and original a man that he had something in him of what makes the founder of a religion. Many of his followers were more or less ready, in their hearts, to treat him as the founder of a religion. They were willing to let the Franciscan spirit escape from Christendom as the Christian spirit had escaped from Israel. They were willing to let it eclipse Christendom as the Christian spirit had eclipsed Israel. Francis, the fire that ran through the roads of Italy, was to be the beginning of a conflagration in which the old Christian civilisation was to be consumed. That was the point the Pope had to settle; whether Christendom should absorb Francis or Francis Christendom. And he decided rightly, apart from the duties of his place; for the Church could include all that was good in the Franciscans and the Franciscans could not include all that was good in the Church.

There is one consideration which, though sufficiently clear in the whole story, has not perhaps been sufficiently noted, especially by those who cannot see the case for a certain Catholic common sense larger even than Franciscan enthusiasm.

Yet it arises out of the very merits of the man whom they so rightly admire. Francis of Assisi, as has been said again and again, was a poet; that is, he was a person who could express his personality. Now it is everywhere the mark of this sort of man that his very limitations make him larger. He is what he is, not only by what he has, but in some degree by what he has not. But the limits that make the lines of such a personal portrait cannot be made the limits of all humanity. St. Francis is a very strong example of this quality in the man of genius, that in him even what is negative is positive, because it is part of a character. An excellent example of what I mean may be found in his attitude towards learning and scholarship. He ignored and in some degree discouraged books and book-learning; and from his own point of view and that of his own work in the world he was absolutely right. The whole point of his message was to be so simple that the village idiot could understand it. The whole point of his point of view was that it looked out freshly upon a fresh world, that might have been made that morning. Save for the great primal things, the Creation and the Story of Eden, the first Christmas and the first Easter, the world had no history. But is it desired or desirable that the whole Catholic Church should have no history?

It is perhaps the chief suggestion of this book

that St. Francis walked the world like the Pardon of God. I mean that his appearance marked the moment when men could be reconciled not only to God but to nature and, most difficult of all, to themselves. For it marked the moment when all the stale paganism that had poisoned the ancient world was at last worked out of the social system. He opened the gates of the Dark Ages as of a prison of purgatory, where men had cleansed themselves as hermits in the desert or heroes in the barbarian wars. It was in fact his whole function to tell men to start afresh and, in that sense, to tell them to forget. If they were to turn over a new leaf and begin a fresh page with the first large letters of the alphabet, simply drawn and brilliantly coloured in the early medieval manner, it was clearly a part of that particular childlike cheerfulness that they should paste down the old page that was all black and bloody with horrid things. For instance, I have already noted that there is not a trace in the poetry of this first Italian poet of all that pagan mythology which lingered long after paganism. The first Italian poet seems the only man in the world who has never even heard of Virgil. This was exactly right for the special sense in which he is the first Italian poet. It is quite right that he should call a nightingale a nightingale, and not have its song spoilt or saddened by the terrible tales of Itylus

M

or Procne.   In short, it is really quite right and
quite desirable that St Francis should never
have heard of Virgil.   But do we really desire
that Dante should never have heard of Virgil?
Do we really desire that Dante should never have
read any pagan mythology?   It has been truly
said that the use that Dante makes of such fables
is altogether part of a deeper orthodoxy; that
his huge heathen fragments, his gigantic figures
of Minos or of Charon, only give a hint of some
enormous natural religion behind all history
and from the first foreshadowing the Faith.   It
is well to have the Sybil as well as David in the
Dies Irae.   That St. Francis would have burned all
the leaves of all the books of the Sybil, in exchange
for one fresh leaf from the nearest tree, is perfectly
true; and perfectly proper to St. Francis.   But
it is good to have the Dies Irae as well as the
Canticle of the Sun.

By this thesis, in short, the coming of St.
Francis was like the birth of a child in a dark
house, lifting its doom; a child that grows up
unconscious of the tragedy and triumphs over it
by his innocence.   In him it is necessarily not
only innocence but ignorance.   It is the essence
of the story that *he* should pluck at the green
grass without knowing it grows over a murdered
man or climb the apple-tree without knowing
it was the gibbet of a suicide.   It was such an
amnesty and reconciliation that the freshness

of the Franciscan spirit brought to all the world. But it does not follow that it ought to impose its ignorance on all the world. And I think it would have tried to impose it on all the world. For some Franciscans it would have seemed right that Franciscan poetry should expel Benedictine prose. For the symbolic child it was quite rational. It was right enough that for such a child the world should be a large new nursery with blank white-washed walls, on which he could draw his own pictures in chalk in the childish fashion, crude in outline and gay in colour; the beginnings of all our art. It was right enough that to him such a nursery should seem the most magnificent mansion of the imagination of man. But in the Church of God are many mansions.

Every heresy has been an effort to narrow the Church. If the Franciscan movement had turned into a new religion, it would after all have been a narrow religion. In so far as it did turn here and there into a heresy, it was a narrow heresy. It did what heresy always does; it set the mood against the mind. The mood was indeed originally the good and glorious mood of the great St. Francis, but it was not the whole mind of God or even of man. And it is a fact that the mood itself degenerated, as the mood turned into a monomania. A sect that came to be called the Fraticelli declared themselves the true sons

of St. Francis and broke away from the compromises of Rome in favour of what they would
have called the complete programme of Assisi.
In a very little while these loose Franciscans
began to look as ferocious as Flagellants. They
launched new and violent vetoes; they denounced
marriage; that is, they denounced mankind.
In the name of the most human of saints they
declared war upon humanity. They did not
perish particularly through being persecuted;
many of them were eventually persuaded; and
the unpersuadable rump of them that remained
remained without producing anything in the least
calculated to remind anybody of the real St.
Francis. What was the matter with these people
was that they were mystics; mystics and nothing
else but mystics; mystics and not Catholics;
mystics and not Christians; mystics and not men.
They rotted away because, in the most exact
sense, they would not listen to reason. And St.
Francis, however wild and romantic his gyrations
might appear to many, always hung on to reason
by one invisible and indestructible hair.

The great saint was sane; and with the very
sound of the word sanity, as at a deeper chord struck
upon a harp, we come back to something that was
indeed deeper than everything about him that
seemed an almost elvish eccentricity. He was
not a mere eccentric because he was always
turning towards the centre and heart of the

maze; he took the queerest and most zigzag short cuts through the wood, but he was always going home. He was not only far too humble to be an heresiarch, but he was far too human to desire to be an extremist, in the sense of an exile at the ends of the earth. The sense of humour which salts all the stories of his escapades alone prevented him from ever hardening into the solemnity of sectarian self-righteousness. He was by nature ready to admit that he was wrong; and if his followers had on some practical points to admit that he was wrong, they only admitted that he was wrong in order to prove that he was right. For it is they, his real followers, who have really proved that he was right and even in transcending some of his negations have triumphantly extended and interpreted his truth. The Franciscan order did not fossilise or break off short like something of which the true purpose has been frustrated by official tyranny or internal treason. It was this, the central and orthodox trunk of it, that afterwards bore fruit for the world. It counted among its sons Bonaventura the great mystic and Bernardino the popular preacher, who filled Italy with the very beatific buffooneries of a Jongleur de Dieu. It counted Raymond Lully with his strange learning and his large and daring plans for the conversion of the world; a man intensely individual exactly as St. Francis was intensely individual. It counted Roger Bacon, the first naturalist whose experiments with light and water had all the luminous quaintness that belongs to the beginnings of natural history; and whom even the most material scientists have hailed as a father of science. It is not merely true that these were great men who did great work for the world; it is also true that they were a certain kind of men keeping the spirit and savour of a certain kind of man, that we can recognise in them a taste and tang of audacity and simplicity, and know them for the sons of St. Francis.

For that is the full and final spirit in which we should turn to St. Francis; in the spirit of thanks for what he has done. He was above all things a great giver; and he cared chiefly for the best kind of giving which is called thanksgiving. If another great man wrote a grammar of assent, he may well be said to have written a grammar of acceptance; a grammar of gratitude. He understood down to its very depths the theory of thanks; and its depths are a bottomless abyss. He knew that the praise of God stands on its strongest ground when it stands on nothing. He knew that we can best measure the towering miracle of the mere fact of existence if we realise that but for some strange mercy we should not even exist. And something of that larger truth is repeated in a lesser form in our own relations with so mighty a maker of history. He also is a giver of things we could not have even thought of for ourselves; he also is too great for anything but gratitude. From him came a whole awakening of the world and a dawn in which all shapes and colours could be seen anew. The mighty men of genius who made the Christian civilisation that we know appear in history almost as his servants and imitators. Before Dante was, he had given poetry to Italy; before St. Louis ruled, he had risen as the tribune of the poor; and before Giotto had painted the pictures, he had enacted the scenes. That great painter who began the whole human inspiration of European painting had himself gone to St. Francis to be inspired. It is said that when St. Francis staged in his own simple fashion a Nativity Play of Bethlehem, with kings and angels in the stiff and gay medieval garments and the golden wigs that stood for haloes, a miracle was wrought full of the Franciscan glory. The Holy Child was a wooden doll or bambino, and it was said that he embraced it and that the image came to life in his arms. He assuredly was not thinking of lesser things; but we may at least say that one thing came to life in his arms; and that was the thing that we call the drama. Save for his intense individual love of song, he did not perhaps himself embody this spirit in any of these arts. He was the spirit that was embodied. He was the spiritual essence and substance that walked the world, before anyone had seen these things in visible forms derived from it : a wandering fire as if from nowhere, at which men more material could light both torches and tapers. He was the soul of medieval civilisation before it even found a body. Another and quite different stream of spiritual inspiration derives largely from him; all that reforming energy of medieval and modern times that goes to the burden of *Deus est Deus Pauperum*. His abstract ardour for human beings was in a multitude of just medieval laws against the pride and cruelty of riches; it is to-day behind much that is loosely called Christian Socialist and can more correctly be called Catholic Democrat. Neither on the artistic nor the social side would anybody pretend that these things would not have existed without him; yet it is strictly true to say that we cannot now imagine them without him; since he has lived and changed the world.

And something of that sense of impotence which was more than half his power will descend on anyone who knows what that inspiration has been in history, and can only record it in a series of straggling and meagre sentences. He will know something of what St. Francis meant by the great and good debt that cannot be paid. He will feel at once the desire to have done infinitely more and the futility of having done anything. He will know what it is to stand under such a deluge of a dead man's marvels, and have nothing in return to establish against it; to have nothing to set up under the overhanging, overwhelming arches of such a temple of time and eternity, but this brief candle burnt out so quickly before his shrine.